W9-AWN-089

literary arts Porcupine magazine

Volume 6
Issue 1

Porcupine Staff

Editors:

W. A. Reed	Barbara Joosse	Judy Bierma
Chris Skoczynski	Vicki Reed	Brandon Lewis

Graphic Design:
   Lynne Palombi

Distribution:
   Bernhard DeBoer, Inc.

Cover Art

Front Cover: Wild Flowers, 22" x 24" Pastel
         by Christopher Copeland

Back Cover: Autumn Haze, 16" x 20" Pastel
         by Christopher Copeland

Afterward in Two Rivers by Kathryn Gahl (page 130) appears as a tribute to the events of September 11, 2001, forever etched in our hearts and minds.

Acknowledgements

Porcupine Literary Arts Magazine is supported, in part, by a grant from the Kohler Foundation.

We also thank these individuals, without whom publication of this issue would not have been possible:
   Sarah McEneany   Patricia Zuelsdorf   Charles Radtke

Porcupine is a not for profit literary arts magazine published semiannually in Cedarburg, Wisconsin 53012 (P.O. Box 259).

Phone: 262-375-3128 email: Ppine259@aol.com
Website: http://members.aol.com/ppine259

There is no distinct edge between art forms, between the artists' works and lives, between one artist's work and another's. Artists connect people to each other, people to the earth, the present to the past and future.

Visual art work and poetry, short fiction and other literary manuscripts will be given prompt attention, but must be accompanied by a self-addressed, stamped envelope. One-time publishing rights have been granted to Porcupine. All copyrights are retained by the authors.

Porcupine is produced on a Macintosh® computer system using Quark Express™.
The text is set in 10 pt. Sabon Roman and Italic, with headlines and captions in Sabon and various weights and styles of Formata.

©2001 Porcupine Literary Arts Magazine
International Standard Book Number: 0-9663121-6-3

Featured Artist
Interview by Barb Joosse

Flora Langlois:
What She Sees

Photo by Sarah McEneany

Flora Langlois was born in Costa Rica. Following her mother's early introduction to art, music, and serious literature, she was sent to the United States where she continued her art education at Immaculate Heart College in Hollywood, California and then Layton School of Art in Milwaukee. She currently paints at her home in Thiensville, Wisconsin.

*"As adults, we have lost that equality of belief
in what we see and what we don't."*
Paul Zelinsky

Flora Langlois is a small person, brown and nut-like. At 73, she has the bird-bright eyes and smooth-skinned look of a young girl. Her conversation is guileless, and she speaks just above a whisper. People often make a mistake about Flora. They think she *is* small.

Flora says there are people who don't understand her work. They walk through a gallery, not knowing the tiny, inconspicuous woman sitting nearby, is the artist. They glance at her paintings— the detailed landscapes and otherworld creatures— and believe them ephemeral, gauzy. They believe her work inconsequential and pass it by.

But there are others. For those, Flora's art snags something deep down, like a fishhook that drags on the bottom of a lake. And for a reason they may not know, they can't walk away. Flora watches them, watching.

"Women in Costa Rica are decorative."

Flora Maria Saenz was born in Costa Rica. Her father was a student of nature, and took particular delight in raising bees. He was also a wood-carver, highly skilled and expressive. He was also a wealthy industrialist, whose factory produced salt-glazed ceramics— floor tiles, fireplace tiles, sewage pipes. "Dad was the mischievous one. He had a sense of life." Flora's own eyes dance with delight and you see, in them, her father's reflected warmth.

Her mother was different. "Mother grew up in a very formal home. She was serious, introverted, mystical." When Flora's parents were ready to build a home, it was her mother who had the artistic vision and telling instructions. "First, before the house was even begun, she had an eight-foot wall built all around the property. She wanted complete privacy, no one looking at her, she looking at no one."

Although Costa Rica is steeped in Catholicism, Flora's parents weren't religious. "Mother didn't go to church. She was a mystic. My dad said the church was for women." Nonetheless, Flora's parents sent her to an all-girls' school, run by French nuns. "It was large, took up a whole block, and had high walls, like a fortress. There were only two entrances. You'd go to the door and ring the bell. A nun would open a little window and look out, and then let you in." More walls.

Costa Rican culture dictates that its women be decorative, an expectation serving as yet another wall. "Parents— and then husbands— do everything. I never even knew how to buy a dress. Mother picked out my clothes and my friends. When you're chaperoned like this, how can you be your own person?

"Most Costa Rican ladies concentrate on giving tea parties. All my childhood girlfriends are like that. Their husbands dote on them, buy them jewelry. They're interested in lavish entertaining."

Later, in the early 1980's, Flora confronted all these restrictions through her art. "I wanted to get rid of the walls. I didn't want to be closed up."

But a wall provides something besides exclusion. It creates interior spaces. Flora's mother, herself a formidable artist, had a studio on the second floor. "There was a terrace there, outside her studio, where she would disrobe and sun bathe." Flora's mother designed many arches in their home, narrow curved arches that reminded her of the Italian artist, D'Anuncio. These words were inscribed above the arch that led to her studio: "Art is lasting and life is short." Inside the studio, Flora and her mother painted side by side. Though her mother didn't say it, she implied approval by allowing her daughter to share this most-sacred space. It was through this narrow canal, then, that Flora's art was born.

Flora's mother served soup every evening. "We would eat in the dining room, very formal, with a white tablecloth. Mother ladled out the soup to our guests, like a ceremony. She would ladle soup from the tureen into other people's bowls."

And so, Flora's mother ladled soup into her bowl. Art. Music. Serious literature. Theater. "We (her brother, Guido, and Flora) were brought up different," she said. "Mother had a different vision for me." Her mother said, "Someday I want you to go to the United States. And someday I want you to be a great artist." Already, in young Flora, dualities had been formed. A society that expects decorative women/a mother who raised a passionate artist. Restrictive Catholicism/ spiritual mysticism.

As promised, Flora's mother sent her to the United States, where she continued her art education at Immaculate Heart College, in Hollywood, California and then Layton School of Art in Milwaukee. "Here, women are more independent," and her parents were far away, so Flora began to take pleasure in making her own decisions, and performing the small tasks that create a

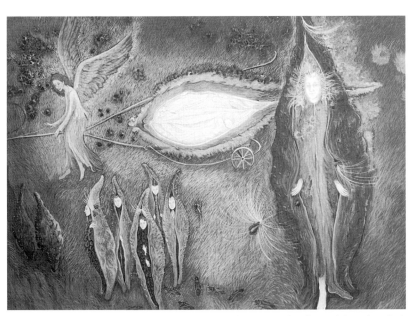

Faith in a Seed Milkweed (Seed Series)
Silverpoint and Acrylic by Flora Langlois

La Muerte
Silverpoint by Flora Langlois

self-determined woman. In Milwaukee, Flora met her future husband, Leslie Langlois, who was attending medical school. "When I met Leslie, my mother worried about him. 'Will he know what to do with Flora, who has been brought up to be dependent?' But I was looking forward to doing it all myself." When Leslie and Flora were living in New York, her brother, Guido, came to visit. Flora's son, Jeffrey, had been born, and now she was carrying a laundry basket with wet diapers. Guido snatched the basket away from her. "I can not imagine my sister carrying a laundry basket!"

But there was a conflict of expectation in Guido, too. "He had taken an aptitude test for college (Loyola University), and they determined that he was shining in all the arts. Father wanted him to study business, but mother prevailed. He went to the New England Conservatory of Music." But his education was interrupted. "Father was dying and called for Guido to return and run the family business." After their father died, Guido did what was necessary, "but there was a huge knot in his stomach."

Flora laughed, her father's puckish nature twinkling in her eyes. "But life has a way of offering opportunities. After a while, someone asked him to teach an acting class at the University in Costa Rica. He was in theater then." Thus restored Guido's involvement in art, now a lifelong devotion. In Costa Rica, in fact, he's known as "Mr. Culture" because of his subsequent appointment as the first Minister of Culture by then-president, Jose Figueres.

Flora returns to Guido's estate in Costa Rica every year, usually for 2-3 months, always to paint. The Saenz name is very important in Costa Rica. Theirs is a family of political, economic and cultural importance. Guido's estate is large and beautiful. In Costa Rica, Flora is embraced by the rainforest, her family, and the considerable collected art of her father, mother, brother and her. People attend to her needs. It isn't that way here, of course. An artist's income isn't vast, and there are no "people" to serve you. Flora's friends wonder why she doesn't just stay there?

A Lush Journey

Although Flora's husband, Leslie, had a penetrating intellect, he was frail. "Leslie was not a healthy man. A great soul and a great mind. And because I was brought up with nuns, so mystic! — the body part was not so important. I knew there was something about the physical, but it was not there. Yet these were definitely growing years for me. He showed me a lot of other religions, other nationalities. When he died, it was a great loss to me in the area of the intellect, but as a woman, I didn't think I really knew what life was about." Flora became a widow after ten years of marriage.

"I married again in 1975 (Francis Pauls) but I was thinking in terms of security, a good man. We didn't have much in common but sports. My friend said, 'but it's too much time between sports.'" The marriage lasted only two years.

But in the same way Flora had embraced her independent nature years before, she now began to embrace sensuality. This lush journey began when she moved to Door County, shortly after the breakup of her second marriage, and met Scott Chobot in 1978. Scott, twenty years her junior, was a Viet Nam vet who lost both legs in the war. "Scott had mood swings, would sometimes go outside and pound his fists on trees. But he was always gentle and loving to me." Scott was very independent,

The Storm
Acrylic by Flora Langlois

wanted to do everything despite having two prostheses. "One day I saw Scott walking in his wooden legs in the field behind my house. The grass was very tall and he had to move slowly, with great difficulty. He was picking flowers for me!" Flora's relationship with Scott was romantic and loving.

Later, Flora became involved with another man, Frank, a tempestuous relationship that blew hot and cold, on and off, for ten years. Frank had a dark side. Flora sensed this early in their relationship, but they were companionable, and the highs in their relationship were so good. Eventually, though, he turned his darkness toward her through emotional abuse and finally, physical abuse. Flora ended her relationship with Frank when the physical abuse began, but she still looks back. "We were so much alike. It makes me wonder if I have a dark side, too." It took Flora a long time to understand a violent nature and its limitations, and finally to confront it. This took courage of an extraordinary measure.

Together, Flora's relationships with these men were companionable, intellectual, passionate, empathic, romantic and conflicted. They played out all the human emotions, and acquainted Flora with her own physical and emotional range. Confronting expectations, creating a world of her own choosing, resolving dualities, embracing sensuality and confronting violence... all these have given Flora substance. It's this substance that gives her art weight, even when the subject matter appears to be "ethereal." You cannot show light without shadow.

Her Art

All the complex realities of Flora's life are expressed in her art. With unflinching courage, she paints the world that *is*. Reality. But of course, for a powerful woman, reality is two things—what is seen and what is unseen. "The seen" is reflected in the exterior world, the one that nourishes Flora: Nature. "The unseen" is reflected in the interior world, the one that gives spice to the nourishment: Her inner self. But how do you paint what is not seen? How do you express the sweep of dreams, emotions and yearnings in two paltry dimensions?

Color, of course, and form. Those things express emotion. But might there be a way to combine the exterior world and the interior world? South American authors have created a literary genre that captures both, sometimes called Magic Realism, like in the novel, *Like Water for Chocolate*. But it's hard to maintain the delicate balance between the seen and unseen. If the work is too realistic, the reader will not suspend disbelief. And if the work is too fantastic, the reader isn't involved, doesn't care.

Flora Langlois paints the world of Magic Realism with masterful strokes. She moves effortlessly between both dimensions of reality. Not all of her paintings are within this genre, but all of them have been influenced by it.

The lush Costa Rican rainforest formed Flora, which is perhaps, why nature continues to feed her now. "Anything that has to do with nature, I love. I tell my students to bring a magnifying glass to school and look closely at things. You see the magic and perfection of the simplest things. Like clover! It has little red veins. Nature is so perfect."

So sometimes Flora allows natural things to stand alone, without the "magic" interpretation. These paintings are almost always landscape. Some have an "illuminated border," a technique Flora loves because of her fascination with the Middle Ages. While there may not be a strong metaphorical content, there's still the undercurrent of magic. Nature, itself, is magic, is it not? And Flora treats natural things with particular reverence, giving landscape a mystical glow as if it, too, has a soul.

Other work is strongly metaphorical. This work usually deals with Flora's inner self, the artist's struggle to understand. For an artist, it's questions rather than answers that give work energy. So Flora examines the psyche's inner questions deeply, each painting in a series a look from another angle. "I love to do series."

In one series, Flora examines her mother— life, death, art and influence. Most of these were done around the time of her mother's death, between 1980 - 1984. In *Searching for Oil for the Lamp of the Sacred*, Flora had found her mother wandering through the living room at night, disoriented. She asked what she was looking for? Her mother said, "I'm searching for oil for the lamp of the sacred." Was this evocative reply the ramblings of an

Searching for Oil for the Lamp of the Sacred
Silverpoint with tinted ground
by Flora Langlois

old woman, or was it something deeply mystical? Flora painted this scene and imbued it with both interpretations.

Another is titled *La Muerte*. "When Mother died, we wanted to be with her in our home. Usually in Costa Rica, you die and are buried that afternoon. So it was unusual for us to want to keep her. Close family came. We tied a little ribbon around her jaw and head. I had a dream that night. Mother looked so peaceful. She was very young looking. When you die, all the muscles loose their strain. Very beautiful. So I had a vision of Mom then, her spirit taking off like a bird. It was very very vivid. I painted it right away."

When Flora's relationship with Frank raised other questions, she resolved those issues in her art. *The Storm*, looks at the effect of Frank's mercurial moods on Flora, herself. In this drawing, a woman's chest and heart are exposed. Her blood has turned to leaves, blown by the wind. The drawing is shadowed on the right, lighter on the left. Flora said, "There's a tree on the dark side. It looks like an artery— arteries are also seen on the woman's arms. The roots are exposed in the tree, but it's still hanging on."

While much of Flora Langlois' work is personal, most of it isn't so intimate. "Some people call me the Witch of the Woods because I'm always collecting things. I'm always picking up rocks, pods, seeds. I keep a bucket in the car. Not long ago, I was driving and looking. My friend said, "Flora! Would you *please* let me drive?"

Several years ago, Flora did a seed series. Seeds, perhaps for someone who watches the road instead of the forest, are not such a big deal. Necessary maybe, because they're the start of life. But Flora's seed paintings do much more than record botanical detail. In studying seeds, she has used a magnifying glass to look at the seen and unseen possibilities. And for those of us who aren't so comfortable with the unseen world, she illuminates this lush interior world. Flora Langlois' seed series captures the mystical essence of seeds. "Seeds became like little people, little souls." There were a dozen paintings in Flora's seed series, and all of them have a quality of light (hope) as well as darkness (despair). It is the interplay that gives them such power. While nature is the subject, humanity is the implication. An artist knows herself best, so when a woman emerges from the shroud of a milkweed pod, we think of Flora being reborn. The miracle of seeds, of course, is propagation. And the miracle of Magic Realism is that the emerging woman becomes not the artist— but us.

At 73, Flora has found the particular joy that comes from self-acceptance. She's at peace with herself and the world. Her art, always a reflection of her inner self, bursts from its core, as if the frame cannot hold it in.

Her newest series, *Interior Gardens*, captures Flora's exuberant joy as well as her source of inspiration, nature. "I have so much feeling for natural things. (The series is) a new way of expression, where my thoughts are. Ideas are coming out of my head." All the paintings are of women. "Yes," Flora said. "Because they're all me."

Some paintings are of women outside. Some are inside. All contain Magic Realism. *Interior Gardens* is personal without being intimate, and like all great personal work, it transcends the personal and becomes universal. Everyone loves natural things. Nature inspires us all.

Follow Your Bliss depicts a woman in a bedroom. She sits in a chair, in front of a window, and reads a book titled... *Follow Your Bliss*. There's a strong sense of movement in the painting, perhaps because the woman, like Flora, longs to be outside. Her hair floats upward and reaches toward the window— a tendrilled, bountiful mess, tangled with insects, flowers and otherworld creatures. Meanwhile, a tree outside reaches toward the woman. Its willow-like branches look much like the woman's hair, and lure her outside. The longing creates tension and reflects the yearning in us all.

Bees

Flora's life itself is full of metaphor. Sometimes it smacks her between the eyes. The first thing Flora said when I began our interview was unusual. "I've never been afraid of bees."

"My father had beehives in the yard. He liked science. Had snakes in jars, a collection. One day, when I was three years old,

Catching Dreams
Acrylic by Flora Langlois

I disappeared. No one could find me. They looked outside and saw me standing in the beehives. I had short, curly hair, and it was *full of bees*! Father put on his hat with a veil and went outside to rescue me, but I didn't have a single bite.

"I'm never afraid of bees. I let them buzz around my head and they never bite. Well, except for one time. I was painting a flower. A bee came up to the painting, like it was going into the flower, and I laughed. 'You might as well go away. These are not real.'" Flora laughed. "And it bit me."

Much later she told me about having an idea that very day. "This morning, I had an idea in the car. I don't feel safe to have a notebook to write down my ideas, but sometimes they leave. I don't know what the idea was this morning. Now it's gone. But you know, ideas buzz around my head all the time," said Flora, whose name comes from Latin, and is the Roman goddess of flowers.

Are bees her talisman? "No. No. I used to think a hawk. But then I thought a hummingbird. One day a hummingbird hovered right in front of my head and looked at me. Just like that.

"No. Not bees."

One day, Flora was in her car, driving. "There was a bee in there and he was cleaning himself. I was so *fascinated!* There he was, rubbing his little legs on his body. So I watched. I crashed the car into a retaining wall." She laughed. "It cost $2,000 damage. Then the police came. 'What happened?' they asked. I said, 'There was a bee in the car.' Of course, they assumed I was afraid of the bee, which of course I wasn't. I couldn't tell them I was watching it, could I?" It is funny, isn't it, that something as small as a bee could break down a wall.

Barb Joosse, Cedarburg, Wisconsin, has published 22 books for children including *Mama, Do You Love Me?, Alien Brain Fryout,* and *I Love You the Purplest.* Her most recent book is *Ghost Wings,* illustrated by Giselle Potter and published by Chronicle Books.

Anne Silver

Poetry

Mystery Kiss

She fell for the artist standing at his easel in the park.
His sexy eye focused on his perpendicular thumb.
Jealous of the posing apple, blue shawl and iris,
and sick with love, she shed her blouse,
skirt, skin and every bone
and kissed his mouth with her invisible lips.
He thought it was a strange breeze
plus something else he must explore
and filled the sky in his still life
with arrows and abandoned clothes.

Let Them Eat!

If people were cakes, I'd be pound with an almond slit.
My brother, devil's food.
My mother, angel.
Dad, upside down.
My cousin, sponge.
And my last boyfriend who cheated
at cards and love, crumb.

Eat!

My love for him is a chocolate mousse pie
ten inches high, a yard wide.
I give him the tiniest, silver spoon.

News

I awake and find he is a folded newspaper
headline spread across the pillow:
I LOVE YOU.
Climbing onto him to be wrapped,
I'm a fish in the market.

Anne Silver, Marina del Ray, California, is a recent survivor of breast cancer. She has been published or has work forthcoming in *Nimrod, Spoon River,* and *Plainsongs*.

Barry Ballard

Poetry

First Morning

There's an inscription inside that cloud hinged
on the horizon, sealed like an inverted
cuneiform wedged sideways into the earth.
It's written out of yesterday's deep-lying
faults, from the thirst of each mistake. And in
hours it will reach me as the content sheds
its color in streaming burn-off, each word
untangled in pure thought before dying.

And so I take what I can of it now,
and anticipate what I hope it can be
when it splits into a millennium
of suppositions, or when it somehow
concentrates its meaning into one key
embryo of dew, gleaming against the sun.

Aurora Borealis

Here I am again, begging God for life,
a teardrop bubble of sometimes weary
magnetism bending this feather of shape
in solar wind. And all my questions
glowing in wide curtains of green-gray sky,
orchestrated swells of confusion and need
singeing this ash-like memory that accumulates.
And I sweep my roar through this stygian

flood of darkness in zodiacal light,
with something of first hope from our parent
nebula, a tapering cone that rests
on both horizons with its path stretched tight
from the backscattered sun, pouring its essence
through every uncertainty that I confess.

Barry Ballard, Burleson, Texas, has a strong preference for writing contemporary sonnets. "I have adopted a phrase that I borrow from N. Scott Momaday about reinventing the sacred. These poems speak to that." His first collection entitled *Green Tombs to Jupiter* won the 2000 Snail's Pace Poetry Prize from Siena College.

Anne Pierson Wiese

Poetry

Shine

The Spanish have a word, *perdedor*,
beautiful loser, one who rides at windmills,
waits in the bar for someone he knows will
not arrive, year after year, drunk and warm,

sufficiently stern past two AM to warn
that those who strive for the ideal
do not succeed. What's at stake is liquid—
liberally flung it travels farther

than imagination— what we call love,
the distance from the front door to the car
and back, these easy trips are not abrupt
enough to spill our souls. When darkness comes,
will we have no word to choose that flaw in us
which loosed unlooses a facade of stars?

You Are Here

They say I could travel to Africa
on four hundred milligrams of quinine
a day— two pills methodically aligned
between my plate and my water glass—

isosceles triangle, mathematics
equation, white chalk drawn on green reminds
me that in the process of divining
hope we have to make a diagram, map

of my body, pale secret continent
unnavigated before pain began—
hot rain, dry frost, whichever way you went
there was a bone crack you could not cross, sand
so deep you could not walk, one message sent
back: *am alone now, cusp edge of God's hand.*

Anne Pierson Wiese, Brooklyn, New York, writes: "I am having fun with sonnets." Her recent work has been published in *High Plains Literary Review, The Journal, The South Dakota Review, Literal Latte, Web del Sol, The Ledge,* and *The Saint Ann's Review*. She is a 2002 Pushcart Prize nominee.

Charlotte McCaffrey

Poetry

Wind Chill Factor

When my grandmother had hers removed,
she complained of the cold.
We wandered down the windy beach in the evening.
You don't think of that beforehand.
She crossed her arms over the flat plains
of her chest as she spoke.
Our walks were always after the sun had gone down.
Post radiation, the bright light of day was forbidden.
Her cool, dark bedroom was forever fringed
with the hats she would take off and toss.
Within the mahogany dresser drawers,
I glimpsed the bulky white contraptions
she strapped on each morning
after shooing us out and closing the door.
Even her daughters were left outside.

My aunt had to forfeit only one.
Do you want to see?
she asked, six months after the surgery.
She pulled open her soft, pink nightgown,
revealing herself.
She and I both looked, curiously.
I shrugged, was nonchalant,
but privately thought
that I could have done the job just as well myself
blindfolded with a dull hatchet.
My aunt buttoned up her flannel.
I'm too small to need a prosthesis.
But there are times I look down at myself
and it seems like someone has
made the bed and left off a pillow.

Now it has come down to you,
drifting through the air,
the water, the years,
who knows.
Before surgery, you write on the good one:
NO! DO NOT REMOVE!
and draw arrows to the bad one.
You join a group, write a piece,
tell us all.
Your chemo-bald head
moves through the city
as you bend against the wind
wigless and
without apology.

In Such Form

*First fossil records of the rose date back 3.5 billion years. In 3000
B.C., in what is now Iraq, the Sumerians created the first written
record of the rose.*
　　　　　　　　　　　　　　　—American Rose Society

Two roses
in such form
new to the world
just this spring
yet so well versed
in their field
in their charge to
delight
eyes noses lips

How new
are these roses
their hips
seeming to curve
toward each other
coming up with
the sweet bees who
in vestments of wings
marry them

In the lull of past winters
these two lasted
formless
dormant except
in desire
in their red fleshy petals
they are now universally new
and all of the old winds carry
the swirl of their scents

Charlotte McCaffrey was born in Mobile, Alabama, and moved to California after two
decades in the Midwest. She is a former chef, bartender, and convent worker. Her work has
appeared or is forthcoming in *Carquinez Review, Sojourner,* and *Writers' Forum.*

Oak Nursery (Seed Series)
Silverpoint and Acrylic by Flora Langlois

Robin Merigan
Prose Poetry

The Enamoring

When we first find each other at that small, late-night gathering, it's a mystery's emergence, a sudden bubble bursting from beneath the surface of dark's pool— how have we each *not* known the other for so long? This seems a mystery to those others present as well, who take obvious delight in introducing us.

What is done to my lips & tongue is so done to my mind— both a sweetness & a bite— comfort aside trepidation— an assurance concurrent with a sense of the ominous.

Immediately, I know what it is to fall in love.

& As with any smitten young woman, I must spend as much time with this new presence in my life as possible, even though this proves difficult & impractical— or because. Finding ways to get together are a stone on which I sharpen my underage cunning– each success giving me an exhilarating sense of control unlike any I've known for ages. I am not to be denied.

Fast we are deep. I am atop a horse, a great liquid beast whose strength transports me, whose danger challenges me— I want to gallop at full when all is dark, to sense a rushing over a landscape I can scarcely see, to feel myself carried without knowing precisely to where or even why. & This beast

is untamable— almost as assuredly as I get on for the ride, I am thrown.

Injuries occur. Accrue.

Without apology, it splinters my unsuccessful facades as if brittle clay— worries my bones' sharp edges to dust— carves its name next to mine in the taught, soft canvas of my skin— & with fingers that feel me up from within the pliant realms of my deepest cavities, scoops out of me the things I could never name & deposits them at my side to eat cold in the morning.

But
I am young, thirsty & enamored. Besides, there is a penetrating familiarity to us— a bond that could not be severed without it feeling like amputation.

Robin Merigan, Seattle, Washington, was awarded the Washington Poets Association's William Stafford Award in 1999. Local and national publications include *American Poets and Poetry, Argestes,* and *Black Spring Review.*

Jim Redmond

Poetry

Poem for a Wife

Say for instance there is a tent near a lake under a moon
that strings the world in tinsel. Teenagers drink beer
in the glow of a fire, laugh, carry on about a football game.
A good time. Say then, too, your future wife is there, drunk,
and gets pulled into this tent, the top as silver as the surface of
the lake,
by a boy with a good story. She gets fucked, of course,
has her cheerleader skirt lifted and panties ripped and thinks
the way her head moves back and forth on the canvas will make
her sick. She goes back to the fire, laughs at how the world spins,

wills herself not to vomit. Years later you are with this woman,
outside a bar, say, the parking lot wet with moonlight, the air
velvet against your skin. Inside people light Marlboros and wait
for a country band to rise from the smoke. Suppose *you* have a
good story,
about a barn maybe, or a culvert once fished, and she listens
over Coronas, nods her head, pulls her hair behind her ears,
is quick to smile. She tells about the football game, not the score
she doesn't recall, but the crowd and chill and how Jenny
Amsterdam
yelled hard enough to pee. Say then this story grows inside you,
a pearl of silver, a drop of light from the moon. Ten, fifteen,
twenty years go by and still you cup her face in your hands,
go back to those flickering moments, turn them over like fire.

Jim Redmond, Crystal, Minnesota, works as a juvenile correctional officer in Minnetonka, Minnesota.

Porcupine-cone #2
10" x 12" Black Ash,
Pine Needles, Porcupine Quills
by JoAnne Russo

William Woods

Fiction

Eastbound and Down

I was halfway between Albuquerque and Amarillo when I noticed the noise. At first it sounded like something in the road, the seams in the pavement, but it came too irregularly, not paced apart like the road would have been. I tried not to pay it any mind. Rigs tend to make noise, most that could be figured out, some that couldn't, sounding off for awhile and then disappearing like the ripples a stone makes when dropped in the water, no matter the height.

Instead, I turned up the radio. Hank Williams came in loud over the deep-bored hum of the drive shaft. The CB was set to standby, individual squawks of static coming in every so often. There wouldn't be much in the way of conversation this side of West Texas. The medium haul. The things to avoid on these runs were falling asleep, and any of those bad habits that would keep you awake. There were a full pack of cigarettes on the dash, but most of the foil insert was gone. I had taken to chewing the foil as a way to taste the nicotine without feeling the smoke. It took the edge off of quitting, this habit. The foil bit down deep in my jaw, and I could just get the hint of flavor. It passed the time on these runs as much as smoking used to.

The runs. Compared to the normal hauls, this one was short, six hours door-to-door. Three hours from Albuquerque to Amarillo— another three to Lubbock, straight down. The interstate was quiet; two lanes in each direction, and with no traffic a driver was prone to lose interest and drift. Since '87, when the cattle market dried up and went south, these interior runs had quieted down. No more parking lots snaking back from weigh stations, no more convoys, rigs six feet apart, riding slipstream off the lead. Now it was down to single drivers, trucks half-filled with bailing wire and industrial lubes, small parts for worthless farm equipment or feed grains for the livestock that limped on as pets. It helped to notice things on these runs. The details. They helped to keep you from getting lulled into a wreck.

I checked the wind. Wind out here had a way of building up through the flats, enough to cause a trailer to jackknife on its hitch. Off to the side, the moon played chase through a run of broken sand dunes, a blue sort of chalkiness drifting out of the ground. Now and again the wind kicked up a cloud, dust mostly, and the occasional tumbleweeds. If the wind ran north, the dust cloud would drop off in the gorge that shadowed the interstate, dropping off to some unseen depths before the land pitched upwards. Blowing south, the tumbleweeds would scoot across the interstate. If I played the air brakes right, I'd vaporize them under the axles of my rig. It wasn't safe, jerking the rig like that, but it helped to break up the hours.

Hours until empty was how a rig related its fuel situation to the driver. Not like a passenger car, which told a straight miles-per-gallon story. This way, depending on the weight of the haul, the miles wouldn't change much, not for speed or road conditions. You could wrench the battery of a running diesel and the rig would keep pushing down the road. But now, carrying what I was carrying, I wished there were some faster way to haul, so that I could be done with this run.

Marital aids. At first I was hoping that meant books, *27 WAYS TO TALK TO YOUR SPOUSE*, or some such. No chance. Just crate after crate of little pink contraptions, taking up the whole length of the trailer. Factory-tested, whatever that meant, and pre-loaded with cheap nicad batteries— ready-to-use right out of the box. A solid load, but made up mostly of rubber and sub-grade metals, nothing that gave the rig any footing. The only weight here was my foot pushing the pedal on down to the floor, trying to make Lubbock by daybreak. I kept checking my surroundings for errant gusts of wind.

And then, the noise. It was slight, so much so that I thought it could be something wrong with the tape deck. I turned the radio down, but there it was, quiet, a dull and irregular scraping just loud enough to be heard over the engine. But it was there, a loose shuffle that seemed to be coming from back behind the third axle. I hoped it was a retread, but retreads tended to go all at once, no warning. A split would breathe in between the vulcanized radial and shuck it from the bald tire underneath. I could ignore a retread, could ride as many as six blown tires out to my next stop, but this noise was something different. I couldn't put a name to it. It could have been a slipped load, like some of the crates had broken their ties and were sliding around the trailer. Heavier freight could have torn through the trailer walls, but this one was light, and the danger was small. If they had slipped, I would still ride it out to Lubbock. See, if there were a list of things I didn't ever want to touch, marital aids would have been pretty much at the top of it. But the noise was too mechanical, too much a deep-throated whir, to be anything as simple as a broken bungee cord. There was nothing I could do but wait it out.

Wait. Outside the window, waiting was altogether some other element. You could see time stacked up alongside the cacti. It wasn't something you outlasted, but something that outlasted you, until it was etched down onto the rock face. I could sit there, alone in the rig, and be annoyed by how long the haul took, but six hours didn't rate out here. Hours didn't matter, or days, or even decades. Time out here was erosion. Time would wear you down. The erosion was as clear-cut as the Interstate, and no six hour run to Lubbock would make a difference, wouldn't shift that one grain of sand enough to cause the dunes to collapse. Maybe then something would be discovered in the sand that had learned that same lesson, some fossilized micro-organism from ages back that once traipsed through these parts, some trilobite that fought the algae and bacteria, back when West Texas was an ocean and not a federally mandated empowerment zone. But then, time had come and rolled over the earth, turned that trilobite and the rest of that ocean into the crude that filled the piggyback tanks of my rig. Would there be enough of me left, after a few days out in the sun, to make it down into the ridge? Or would my International make it to the fossil stage?

I think Shelly filled me in on all that. Shelly, my wife, was a fan of the science channels off the satellite feed back at our split-level. It was a gift to myself, that satellite. The thing is, you have to be home to enjoy the pleasures of satellite television. With payments still left to make, it fell to Shelly to inform me that I got my money's worth. Two weekends a month was how often I got to enjoy the privilege of satellite television from the comforts of my own couch. As soon as I walked in the door, Shelly would start filling me in on how Patton used a phantom army to trick the Nazis into thinking the D-Day invasion would come far north of Normandy, or how lamb had no place in the cuisine of Vietnam. For my part, I tried to keep up with her by reading. At truck stops, with the rig sucking power off the generator to keep the diesel from gelling in the gas tanks, I read whatever I could get my hands on off the light from the ten-inch black-and-white tv. Science quarterlies, pulp paperbacks, gun journals. Religious pamphlets handed to me outside of diners. Technical manuals from equipment I would never own. The occasional book on the history of modern combat or the letter column from a skin mag. I would remind her how horses were not native to North America before the Spanish rode them off their galleons, and how the sight of them riding, more than gunpowder or tall ships, made the Conquistadors into gods. On the skin mags, I actually did try to avoid looking at the pictures. There was nothing for me in the sight of those women, bent over couches or tossed onto the floor, legs and arms all akimbo, enjoying themselves occasionally with some of the gadgets presently roped down in the back of my trailer. Or not roped down, as the noise coming from the back had led me to believe.

The noise had grown load enough to kill off my daydreams and I became acutely aware of my surroundings. All at once I was back tooling around some deserted interstate in the ass end of Texas with an unspecified noise that was growing to sound like god playing horseshoes in a dumpster. It was at best a slipped load of marital aids and, at worst, something else. Maybe it was in the drive shaft, something mechanical, and not just a spot of bad diesel. Bad diesel, even that low octane distilled kerosene shit, would have squibbed through the lines by now. This was something altogether different, a cog or a gear or something in the shaft that was bent or broken or even just sitting wrong and was now grinding itself down, by the sound of things, and doing the worst— cutting into the hours. The indicator lights were dark. I thought to downshift and negotiate through the noise at a slower speed, but just pushed the pedal on down to the floor. Sometimes, when an engine started to slip, it helped to go faster, to force the engine back into tune by burning off its gears. I'd burnt through gaskets like this before, and would burn through more if it meant staying on schedule.

The rig was up around a hundred, but the noise kept getting louder, gaining weight and power as I picked up speed. I tried to downshift, but the noise coiled up behind me and started jacking its way up the drive shaft and I knew then that the noise wasn't anything I could outrun. I downshifted as the noise fisted its way up through the hitch and cracked into the cab. The sleeper burst up from behind and I was pelted with stray coffee cups, magazines flattening against the windshield as the bucket seats rocketed forward and I said a quick prayer for five-point seatbelts when suddenly the noise was gone. Dead cold silence, just plain nothing there, and the rig seemed light, as if it had become weightless. The moon had never seemed so white as it did the moment before the trailer jackknifed around the cab and swallowed the moon whole a half-second before the noise blew up around me, next to me, not in any one place but all over. I actually had time to curse—

OH SHIT— before the drive shaft came apart in a splintering cough, the engine bucking on its mounts as the trailer touched back onto the ground. The tires caught just long enough on the slow pitch over to the side to snap the axles and I threw the air brakes, shredding what was left of the drive shaft. The trailer peeled apart with a sound close to fabric tearing and I swore I heard each and every one of the eighteen wheels blow out as the hoses snapped and the hitch stretched and buckled and struggled to stay hooked to the cab. The rig flipped. 12 tons of diesel burning tractor trailer churned down into the interstate and went pinwheeling off to the soft shoulder, and I knew full well that I was going to be found dead by some dipshit state trooper, burnt into the dashboard and surrounded by bits of smoldering dildos, the rig a blot of flash-twisted steel somewhere in the middle of West Texas. The wreck plowed through the dry slush of sand, coming to a stop like something out of a bad Burt Reynolds movie. Then nothing.

Dry showers. I came to and tasted sand, pouring in through the side window. The cab had flipped onto its side. I was hanging a few inches from the windshield, which had spider-webbed and was struggling to hold back the sand from gulping up the cab. The rig was settling into itself, into the ground, trying to see which would give first. I coughed and felt the seat shake behind me. There were slight pains, bruises, by the feel of things, but no broken bones. I sat there, just breathing, before I pulled the release pin on my five-point seatbelts and fell into the cab. The door was covered in sand. How long had I been out? The driver's side window was gone; the sky frosted dark beyond the hole. I thought to stay in the cab. When the night ended, if it ever did, would I disappear along with it? I would have sat there and pondered that one, maybe, had I not just spilt 36 hours worth of diesel fuel onto the interstate. No way was I gonna suffer the burn. I pulled myself out from the cab and got my first look at the wreck.

Under the moon, the wreck appeared like the lime-chalked bodies stumbled over at the end of some decided war. Metal was pressing into itself with a stink as heavy as the sound. Axles turned where they still could as the engine, an angry swarm of bees, lay fogged and choking in the sand. The point where the piggyback tanks had come apart from the cab had gone darker than the sky, soaked with diesel. Crates were scattered throughout the wreck; some half-buried in the sand, others as far back as the interstate. There was no fire, not yet, and diesel, without fumes, meant the risk of an explosion was slight. I hopped down from the cab and felt the sand oily, even through my boots.

A set of tires spun off-center, the axle snapped, on an upturned section of the trailer. Parts of the trailer had started to smoke, thin streams of black smoke pulling lightly from the aluminum. A smolder fire. Metal separating from metal produces heat, and heat feels a need to grow. I kept walking, trying to concentrate on all of the damage but getting sucked into the details. The custom 'truck turner' mudflaps crushed under the pivot joint, or the mangled chrome bumpers, still so bright I could see my reflection. I wanted to see the whole wreck, but could only get the bits and pieces, the same odd way I would marvel at the parking lot during Wal-Mart's discount days and the fall turkey shoot. The road was rubbed black back where the rig had flipped, the tire tracks blossoming into some hideous bean plant. From there, the tracks grew wider and plunged off into the sand. How long had I been out? The trailer was still hitched to the cab, but pulled apart, like taffy. At that moment, the chemical stink of the diesel and the metal flexing into itself, gave the violence of it all, the force it took to rip things apart, a sort of pristine quality. I hit the ground, desperate to puke, but nothing would come up. I sat with my face to the ground and waited for the fit to end.

Something twitched on the ground in front of me. Twitched and rattled. Rattler. Had to be. Even without the Discovery Channel documentary handy, the sound was unmistakable. I had survived a rig spill of epic proportions only to have plowed through a nest of rattlers, and would still be found dead in the morning, bloated instead of burnt, a handful of Staties chuckling over my snakebit corpse, surrounded by smoldering steel and enough dildos to plug up one of them lesbo colleges in Oregon. There were more snakes, dozens and dozens of them. Some were slithering just under the sand. Some were edging out onto the Interstate. There were snakes crawling around and on top of the pieces of debris. I went still. I hoped they would freeze to death before they noticed me, but then, something touched my ankle right above the boot. Snakebit, I dove to the ground, figuring that I was already as dead as the snakes and might as well take a few of them with me. My hands went thrifty through the sand, grabbing for the one that bit me. There were snakes everywhere, all around me, on my thighs, against my back and shoulders, rubbing up in my face. I grabbed one and started bashing its head into the ground; over and over, until it stopped twitching and went still. But something wasn't right. This snake was rubbery. I held the snake up and saw that it wasn't a snake at all. Hhmm. A few of them crates must have broken open during the crash. Dozens of those little pink numbers were vibrating all skittish like in the sand. There must have been hundreds, thousands, but one alone was enough to scare me. The whiz and hum of the fleshy joy-toys grew louder than the sound of the rig's slow death. One of them was hardly a sound, but together the noise was damned disconcerting. I shook off my fright and walked back to the cab, careful not to step on any of the pink buggers. In the dark, they looked downright fleshy. Back at the cab, the CB seemed to be in good shape, but the antenna was buried somewhere under the rig. I grabbed what I could; my old army field jacket, some gloves from the glove box, and zipped up tight. The wind had died off, but it was still cold enough out here that even the snakes and the lesser vermin huddled together for warmth. As I walked away from the cab, the windshield gave, and everything up to the sleeper seat

PORCUPINE

disappeared into the dune. I had heard of people who paid big money to camp out under the Texas sky, had even seen some of them at truck stops, oddly tanned, their campers gleaming like perfect teeth. But none of these men ever had to contend with the sound of a thousand or so vibrating pink gizmos to keep them company. One vibrator, maybe, had drove them out of the house in the first place, sent them to the camping store, away from the misses, but not thousands of them, with a field of sand-soaked diesel nearby. Not that I had much of a choice. It was cold, sure, but colder for those in Lubbock who were waiting for my load to arrive. I dragged a few of the tires away from the wreck, mindful to stay upwind, and fashioned a makeshift couch. I fished my CDL out of my field jacket. A Commercial Drivers License. All a man needs to drive the big rigs. Well, not all. Just what the state needs to see. The picture was old, the face fresher, younger, the signature crisp and bold under the laminate. The ID curled up at the touch of flame from my Zippo. I dropped the burning ID onto the diesel soaked sand. Direct flame will cause diesel to burn even without the fumes. The flame tracked back to the wreck and turned the trailer into a flaming rack of bones, burning what was left off in a belch of toxic smoke. Rubber liquefied, steel molded into itself and spoiled the ground. I sat back and tasted the smoke, sweet, down deep in my lungs. My first cigarette in weeks. Something else I grabbed from the cab. I had tasted metal for the last time. I watched my rig burn, waiting for the lights of the choppers or the state police, anyone, who would spot the flames.

William Woods is a freelance writer with publishing credits including *The Boston Globe* and *Trailbreaker.com*.

Cactus Basket
6" Black Ash, Pine Needles, Cactus Spines
by JoAnne Russo

Terri Brown-Davidson

Poetry

The Wound

Bitch Goddess craves sex-fixes, a blunt-headed cock her needle.
I prefer running, ninety minutes of endorphin-stealing
when I lace up my Nikes, forget I'm "Dr. D"
for clusters of brain-dead froshpeople
who prefer "Mrs." for my moniker,
the halogram I've become reassuring to them, *irreal*
when they conjure me sliding fudge brownies from an oven
I've never learned to navigate,
The Lost One replenishing energy
with M & M cookies scorched black against the pan,
sugar her aphrodisiac as running's becoming mine,
the flex, the egg-shaped knots of my calves scintillating
when I dart down rubbled sidewalk,
dash beside gutters overflowing
with crimped pinkish butts, with wadded cheeseburger wrappers,
up Zero Street to a park where even the swings swing lonely,
their chains rattling rusting
in the frost-trimmed November wind.

I peel down my shorts' edges, fold them against my thighs.
The branches of elms gone dead-gray with silence
a prelude to a winter that'll find me shrunken in my husband's arms,
dreaming the dream of an afterlife
that materializes when he fucks me on graying mindless days
rimmed hazy with sun pasted beigish over clouds.
It's a dream I've had before.
It started when I fell: moving into the Zone, I felt myself suddenly
airborne, launched, spread my arms as if welcoming angels
snow-mounded into Art,
plummeted against the sidewalk,

split my face open to bone shards and bursts of blood.
Shocked, seconds later, I fumbled, still quivering, upright,
the sky swimming glimmer-edged,
painted with bright red eye-movements
and a metallic taste pouring up from shattered bone
directly beneath my tongue— God knows I was fucked.
But flooded, whispering, swallowing, pasting my torn face together
with two trembling hands, I limped home to a crowd of no one,
my Nikes blossoming scarlet
when I stumbled inside, summoned an ambulance, passed out
before it arrived.

That was my first glimpse. Or rather, on the gurney
when the sour-breathed surgeon twisted my face hard right,
threaded in his needle, humming as he stitched,
the fluorescence searing my retinas
though I laughed, hyena-wild, at the gibberish-stupid pain—
"You're hysterical," he said, humming "O Susannah" in between
breath snatches.
"Want some stronger meds?"
I couldn't shake my head. Signalled him with my eyes.
It was then that the man arrived, or first— rather— the house,
a paint-crumbled affair, stalwart as afternoon glare, cornfields
surrounding it
with greenish-black crows sunstruck, brilliant as tin,
glistering between rows, plucking grubs from furrowed dirt,
an overalled man, back rounding to a hump,
leading a heifer toward a barn
sharded with smoky rot: I understood none of it,

don't understand it, still, though it recurs whenever I'm fucked,
sex my adrenaline dream while teaching Freshmen Comp

and the greasy windows shine with leaves glittering
blue-gold-flat as salamanders
then go gray, suddenly, with a light that's no light,
and— though I'm explicating *Cathedral*,
Carver's crowd of testosteroned drunks,
smoking a cig searing flesh beneath ripped-up, ravaged nails—
it's fucking that permeates my cells, bone-marrow, blood,
the way my husband shudders me,
jars my slick thighs apart until he's *in me* up to the throat,
and that's when the Afterlife appears though it makes so little sense
I shiver and run, shiver and run, envisioning it again—
the man in overalls I've never encountered in this lifetime,
my husband's deep groans as he splits my center open,
deposits his pearly sperm-drop somewhere inside my cunt,
all of us thrashing upstream toward some future we can't imagine,
Bitch Goddess to another bed, to another biker,
me to another wound, to better fellatio, to another vision
I can't render with my consciousness but only
with the upthrusting pain that peels my skull back
until I'm wide and empty, drained and joyful,
my sneakered feet pounding *Rapture*.

Terri Brown-Davidson, Lincoln, Nebraska, was recently selected as a Featured Writer by *The Literary Review/Web del Sol*. Her short stories, novel excerpts, and poems have appeared in or are forthcoming from more than six hundred national and international journals. She is currently a lecturer in Creative Writing at the University of Nebraska-Lincoln.

Porcupine #1
10" x 11", Black Ash, Pine Needles,
Porcupine Quills
by JoAnne Russo

Lydia Webster

Poetry

Tracks

I draw a heart in the snow
blank as paper.
I want to tell him
he keeps changing in my poems,
that his mother's cherry lowboy
was restored, that I saved
the antique gift-wrap lining
from the middle drawer—
the wild silver horses
with their yellow pastel streamers:
it came out whole,
a paper box of air.

I dream I'm on his daily train
wrapped in smoke like streamers,
the engine coasts
to the station, holding back
its rumble. Drops of water
fleck the amber
glass, now it's hard
to see the men on the platform,
their forties' overcoats
and hats. I breathe
a cloud on the window
to drag my finger through
the question— where are you?

Present

This woman waits for her lover to awake, takes a deep
breath and sighs— everything is fine, like years ago waking up
on Christmas, lying in her bed in the dark her parents still

asleep and the whole festival of gifts awaited her and she
hesitated to rouse Mom and Dad, she felt so high coasting on
anticipation, at the top of the stairs, she had to wait

for everyone before descending, the tree lights off, but
the tinsel shimmering, snow feathers on the window, the roar
of the big lake, all of them asleep, her brother, her parents,

just her waiting and crouched by the hallway mirror, afraid
of the dark someone who sees her emerald red and alone
in her fullness— biting and tearing into everything.

Lydia Webster lives in New Mexico, and has work forthcoming in *TriQuarterly,*
StoryQuarterly, Fresh Ground, and *Coal City Review.*

Meghan Hickey

Essay

Orchid

My grandparents live in a wooded suburb fifteen miles north of Milwaukee, Wisconsin, on the southwest shore of Lake Michigan. A summer outpost for wealthy urbanites at the turn of the century, the area has since been pie-sliced by developers. Large-scale, Fischer Price-like homes now preside over diminutive lots in artificially genteel, countrified enclaves, while gravel-edged roads wind round too-green lakes. My grandparents' more veteran subdivision demonstrates its solidarity against the newness by holding seasonal festivals, from autumn corn roasts to Christmas caroling to springtime egg hunting to full-blown summer *patriotismos*. Year-round, my grandparents' modest two-level colonial stands in full salute, its white siding, blue trim, and red brick lending it patriotic panache, a star-spangled banner and an Irish Republic tri-color flag flying at jaunty angles on either side of the front door. Grandpa keeps the lawn and bushes trim with his push mower and shears, while Grandma tends aggressively to the rose beds and other more delicate accessories. From the front lawn, you can catch Lake Michigan winking behind their neighbors' homes, a coy reminder that the lake serves as source of water, weather, and direction. *I may not be the ocean*, it seems to say, *but as compass I rival the sun.*

Our family's waterfront walks begin with an obligatory visit to the small, blufftop clearing we call "Grandpa's Lookout," where the cautious naturalist or eager swimmer can gauge the tide and the mood of the lake by its color. A steep gravel path winds from lookout to shore down the face of a ravine, cutting through a small tract of forest that was set aside as a preserve in the 1970s. Turning the bend halfway down the hill, a visitor comes in sight of a small hesitation of water that collects its thoughts, logs, and moss before making its way slowly into the lake. This pond is all that remains of a considerable reservoir whose now-antique concrete dam has slowly resigned itself to water level, providing a flawed crossing to the far bank where a red canoe waits for paddles in the undergrowth. Over time, five larger fragments of this dam have drifted and resettled down the shore in a solemn gathering I once took for a north shore Stonehenge or midwestern Easter Island. The slabs' rough sides and oxidized piping provide ample foothold for anyone seeking mystery at the water's edge.

As a child, I feared that my grandparents' house would make its way down that slope as well— with my grandparents in it. Erosion does threaten the integrity of many nearby properties; several neighbors have expended considerable sums in the attempt to prop up their lakeside bluffs. But erosion also makes for constant transformation: on every visit, the beach reveals a different face. We return to the waterfront with fondness and reverence; it is a living metaphor of our own ongoing transformations. No family gathering is complete without a walk to the lake.

After attending college out of state, I returned to Lake Michigan by way of Chicago— place of my grandpa's childhood and my grandmother's young adulthood, origin of their courtship, and a city for which they harbor a great affection. They interpreted my move as a kind of unspoken tribute to his heritage. As the unofficial family chronicler of my generation, I delighted in the newfound proximity to my mother's parents, both geographically (Milwaukee is but a short drive away) and historically (my first apartment was located within my great aunt's former neighborhood), while the difference in our ages allowed me to pose them questions that their three daughters might consider taboo. It is not surprising, then, that during a recent visit, I was the first to hear a family story that had not before been told:

The day after their first unofficial date, my grandfather sent my grandmother an orchid. The parcel traveled by rail from Chicago to a juncture in north-central Illinois and then by bus to my grandmother's small hometown, where she was visiting her family for Easter. Grandma received a call from the bus depot, which was then housed in the town's only café; she drove downtown to pick up the unexpected package. Five months later, the two joined lives in a ceremony whose 50th anniversary we celebrated only recently.

Despite its apparent importance, the orchid has, until now, made no appearance in family lore, while the humble carnation held floral court, largely in commemoration of my grandfather's very first courting gesture: weeks after they met, he placed a bunch of green carnations on Grandma's office desk St. Patrick's Day (she worked in Personnel; he, in Engineering). Today, on the feast days of his favorite saints, my grandfather bestows upon wife, daughters, and grandchildren a single carnation color-coded according to holy personage (red for Valentine, green for Patrick). None of us, however, had heard the orchid story until it was retold to me half a century later.

At first glance the orchid, a flamboyant hothouse cutting, seems out of place in our home-grown family album. The

Watercolor by Mary Jeanne Larkin

union of my grandfather— a southside Chicago Irish tough and former seminarian— and my grandmother— a citified farmer's daughter and aspiring painter— took place in the post-war forties, before thrift was chic or even optional. Shipping a flower across the state was an extravagant gesture for a man who today wears his sweaters until they unravel and keeps financial records so tight they're waterproof. The act, like the flower itself, was singular and unlikely. I also found it terribly intriguing: how had the orchid remained outside our family tradition?

To investigate this story was to take an amateur's crack at the Sistine Chapel: I'd fill in the gaps, remain as loyal as possible to the original, and forge the rest in colored pencil. Perhaps write a poem. But even a poet's approach to history requires a foundation of actual evidence. Did Grandma expect the flower? Did it change the way she felt about him? Why did Grandpa choose an orchid? Should either of them fail to provide adequate detail, the poet would step in, and memory might be reconstructed.

And so one evening, as the October sun was setting outside my window, I called my grandmother. She answered, I imagine, sitting at the kitchen desk in her tennis socks and shoes, handkerchief wrapped about her head, one leg bouncing, a To-Do list half-checked before her. "I want to ask you more about the Easter orchid. The one Grandpa sent you before you were married."

"What do you want to know?"

I paused. "Did you blush when you'd opened it?"

"Oh, no, I didn't blush."

"Was it on a stem, or in a box?"

"It must have been in a box, because I could tell it was a flower."

"What did you do with it?"

"I wore it to church on Sunday, pinned to my Easter suit."

"Did you change your outfit to match the flower?"

"No. The suit was blue with purple trim. It matched perfectly. We wore hats back then, you know."

51

I saw the orchid, singular, beautiful, fastened to proud cloth, Grandma's bosom trained to attention in a tailored navy suit, her back straight, eyes high, hair tucked neatly beneath a matching hat. I saw pews of nodding headwear and, outside on the lawn, an early garden of straw disks, pillboxes, fruit baskets, bird perches, scarves, and widows' veils, bright against the still-frozen April sky. I saw Grandma returning to her parents' modest but canary yellow two-story home, removing the corsage in the kitchen, and placing it… in a bowl? In a vase? "What did you do with it afterward?"

"I think I wore it home to Chicago."

"On the train?"

"Sure. When you had a flower in those days, you wore it. I probably wore it until it died." She paused. "We didn't see many orchids, you know. How many do you get in a lifetime? Two, maybe three? How many orchids have YOU had?"

"None," I said.

"See. When you get an orchid, you'll know."

At twenty-seven, I have exceeded the ages at which my mother and grandmother reached the milestones of marriage and children. My grandmother considers my "freedom" to be a great responsibility, even a gift, one I suspect she somewhat envies. Grandma stopped painting after the birth of my mother, her first child, and did not seriously return to her paints until her youngest child had left for school. She and Grandpa, however, raised three daughters with noticeable abilities in music, storytelling, and personal reflection: my aunts are professional musicians and song-writers, and my mother is a pianist and a psychologist. In some ways, their work stands as an alternative to landscape and portraiture. My siblings and I (to simplify) include a writer, a musician, and a visual artist; we therefore carry on the tradition as well. Grandma is a most vocal champion, coach and critic of our creative work. Grandpa is a staunch supporter of family members as well, although his emphasis on the literal is quite renowned: a ledger man and former military cadet, he is known for his withering bluntness and remains unwilling to submit his intellect to any kind of cultural hogwash. "What do you poets do, just talk to each other?" he asked me once after reading my work. Still, before sending a poem to any reader or literary magazine, I think of my grandparents, gauging the poem's accessibility and appropriateness by their anticipated reaction: would Grandpa grasp the metaphors? Would Grandma be proud of the piece? Little material has passed that test, I admit.

Both grandparents reflect the environments in which they grew up: she, farmland; he, city. As details of the newly-discovered orchid story unfolded, I grew surer that this flower was a surprisingly appropriate symbol of my grandparents' union and life together, one of small surprises, gentle beauty, and enduring love and faith. It was as though the bloom had arrived again, fifty years later, to thrill and puzzle us. Or at least to puzzle me: my Grandfather, for one, does not consider the orchid story to be an anomaly. "I have always been a flower man," he asserted in a recent letter. At first, this entailed bringing cut flowers to his mother; and now: "Each year at Easter I still give [Grandma] an orchid; each year I give her one green carnation; during the year I try to keep her supplied with one long-stem rose. The flower man. That's my simple language of love."

And what of that first orchid, which my grandmother tells me were primarily "wedding and funeral flowers?" His answer: "I sent an orchid to Grandma to get her attention… it did the trick."

My investigation of the orchid story has enabled me to collaborate with my grandparents in reconstructing a memory scrapbook. Every time we spoke or wrote about the orchid, a new detail would emerge, much to the delight of all. At one point, however, my grandmother, weary of inquiry, demanded, "Can't you just use poetic license?" Grandpa asked me, "Why don't you write about something more interesting?" I thank them for their assistance in shaping this piece and the following poem— my pursuit of whatever truths or beauties lie in their stories, translated to the page.

Meghan Hickey

Poetry

Orchid

Grandma married for an orchid
sent by boxcar from Chicago
on the train she'd ridden the prior day:
slender, erect, useless for planting
in girlhood's passing fields.

Grandpa left the seminary
for the steel mills at eighteen
that his brothers might take
the collar instead, his sister (once,
twice?) decline marriage and
his mother wear black to the grave.

The flower was so exquisite
through the glass, he stopped
to ask its name: *Orchidaceae*,
genus that blooms in canopies
deriving nutrients from air and rain

—the ornament of funerals,
weddings, and wakes. Then
the call came from the depot:
'lo, Miss Sullivan? There's a package.

At church, her modest navy hat
was lost among the nodding pews
of pillboxes and bird perches,
but hers was the only orchid,
pinned to her Easter suit
—a suitor's promise, though

his first gesture was a bunch
of green carnations, nameless, noteless,
on her desk, a prank that has become
his Saint Pat's Day signature. Valentine
now has his own carnation,
dyed a lover's red.

For years, these two have grounded love
in familiars (children, tennis, faith)
where the Common Buckthorn shrub
is exotic, while the orchid hovers
chalice-like behind our family legend—
rococo, singular, sacred, unlikely,

evading the spotlight,
and perhaps for a telling reason:
we may greet orchids in winter
as a promise of the spring, but I trust
no hothouse blossom to forecast
the yield of coming seasons.

Meghan Hickey recently received an MA in Creative Writing from Boston University. Her poetry has previously appeared in *Porcupine* (Volume 3/Issue 2) and can be seen in a forthcoming issue of *The Cream City Review*. She lives in Peabody, Massachusetts.

Christopher Copeland
Portfolio

Passing Storm
20″ x 22″ Pastel by Christopher Copeland

Christopher Copeland was raised in rural Washington County, Minnesota where he grew accustomed to the open and serene landscape. This is where he first developed his interest in the subject matter that is the emphasis of his paintings today. A graduate of the College of Visual Arts in St Paul, Copeland has exhibited his work throughout the country including Boston, New York, Seattle, Minneapolis, Scottsdale and Santa Fe.

Painting outdoors on location, Copeland's main concern is to record nature's transient moments where the light is fleeting and most effective. Using loose but controlled brushwork, he works quickly to capture the atmospheric effects of light, shadow and color as they play on the land. Both emotional and expressive in content, his work is a testament to the mysterious beauty of nature. He currently lives in Stillwater, Minnesota.

Late Afternoon Shadows
24″ x 30″ Oil by Christopher Copeland

Farm Valley
30″ x 36″ Oil by Christopher Copeland

"Working with direct observation from nature I look for abstract compositional elements of the landscape. These may be in the form of an outcropping of trees on the distant horizon or a shadow dividing a sunlit field and a darkened sky. These provide me with the initial geometric arrangement to work from."

Late Season Hay Bales
32″ x 36″ Oil by Christopher Copeland

"Light, color, space and form all become interacting principles in the expression and emotional qualities of the painting."

Autumn Equinox
25" x 26½" Pastel by Christopher Copeland

"The environment plays an important part in establishing an identity in my work. The spareness of the land, hills and space contribute to the sense of place inherent in the painting."

The Height of Color
30" x 34" Oil by Christopher Copeland

"What compels me to keep making art is the tremendous reciprocation between light and land. Each occurrence I find new and exhilarating. To capture that emotional and subjective relationship with the landscape is the reason I paint."

Rain Cloud
21″ x 25″ Pastel by Christopher Copeland

Ben Miller

Poetry

#329

I was crossing 7th Avenue and a couple was coming
the other way. The old man had ashes on his
forehead, the old woman didn't. Her arm was
hooked around his, gently tugging. Behind the two
were others wearing ashes and more Catholics were
streaming out of the church down the block. Had she
waited in the courtyard, next to the statue of St.
Francis, while her husband did his duty? Or had she
guided him to the altar, stepping aside at the very last
minute? The latter seemed most likely. He was far
more feeble than she. Head bowed, feet shuffling.
The belief was his, not hers, and yet she'd capably
assumed partial charge of its management, as a park
ranger does a forest, stamping out the sorry little
sparks, remulching the trails that wind through the
wildflowers and tender grasses.

#331

He sounded like a strangulating animal, this meter
reader from Keyspan Energy. Gisssssssman!
Gisssssssssssman! Gisssssssssssman here! Saturday
morning. My wife and I blinking in the bedroom of
our garden apartment in Brooklyn.
Gisssssssssssssssssman! Gissssman! Gisssssssssssman here!
White shutters on the window, flakes of light on the
slats. A big blue stomach out there, a jiggling belt of
equipment, an aversion to doorbells. Gisssssssman!
Gisssssssssssman! Gisssssssssssman here! Had he simply
tired of being stared at through peep holes like an
offical obscenity? Or was the call inherited from great
grandfather? The way the job had been done before
the malling of New York, in the days of pushcarts and
ponies? Gissssssssman! Gisssssssssssman! Gisssssssssssman
here! The whole neighborhood waking, muttering,
waiting for him to move on. Only he didn't tire easily.
He'd stroll up and down the block for twenty minutes
singing Gisssssssssssman! Gisssssssssssman!
Gisssssssssssman! A free man, pleased when doors
opened and just as happy when not one did.

#350

That morning Jose the security guard was dressed in
a powder blue suit with a white handkerchief poofing
from the pocket. You quit? *Yeh, I quit. Too old to
stand around. Me and the band going to Chicago.
The Six Tops.* His eyes were the whiteyellow of burst
poached eggs, the skin on his neck mottled: patches
of pink, brown, white. He talked fast, shoulder
ducking, body dancing with the words. *We play
Salsa. Blues too. South Side, Gary, Detroit,
Cleveland, going to make the circuit.* And they did,
according to another guard, until five Tops got
homesick for the Bronx and quit one night, leaving
Jose alone and sweating under the strobe light at a
Holiday Inn, neck twitching like a lily in hard rain.

Ben Miller, Brooklyn, New York, has appeared in many publications and new work can
be found in recent or upcoming issues of *The North American Review, Arts & Letters,
Barrow Street, New York Stories,* and *The Little Magazine.* Awards include a creative
writing fellowship from the National Endowment for the Arts.

Onion Dome
10" x 7" Black Ash, Pine Needles
by JoAnne Russo

Joan Payne Kincaid
Poetry

Music Lesson

For Jacqueline Du Pres
"Discipline is the willingness to be bored"

She sat on a ladder for dinner
absent... tilting left/tight subtleness
baptized Catholic I'm catatonic satanical approach to singularity;
who was playing for dancers rhythmically— off kilter fingering
power of large hands and gripping knees
to play the same chord on the cello all day for just right
intonation really is a meditation
summarily negating scenario of
scullery maid image so petite and fitting
as if risin' from the dead huge!
Soup and magic reality.

Her instrument sings life,
working patterns for order   Tremolo
reading to attentive audience
in different positions   Focused
awful trying to cram it in and teach as if who knew?
the hand must be gratified by sixteenth notes   Dorian.

Falling down steps of multiple sclerosis embracing 'cello
sleep before events with which clouds mount
multiplying tragedy the world run by filthy rich villains
one of your first songs Ah Sweet Mystery of Life
at last I've found you, etc. on to disillusionment
practicing activism like an operatic performance to no avail

the mystery of practicing on rainy days in houses with wide porches
and love affairs.

In red silk gown...   like painting cello between lips
doing it to metronomic tic tock be or not to
              be   Attack the thing with violent
instrument   echos   through   old   wooden   walls   of   too   many
late night parties,
music of one's life without war or argument;
terror crawling toward ending at the wrong time...
keep relaxed tissue feel/a certain restraining character
not to reveal everything bowing voice of extravagant passion

Joan Payne Kincaid, Sea Cliff, New York, is a painter, writer, and former opera-concert singer. She is published internationally in magazines, anthologies, and books including: *Understanding the Water* (Kings Estate Press, 1998) and *Skinny Dipping* (Bogg Publications, 1999). She writes: "I have long been drawn to the tragedy of Jacqueline Du Pres; that her brilliant cello career was cut short by Multiple Sclerosis at the height of accomplishment, is a nightmare from which there was no awakening."

A. Loudermilk
　　Poetry

For the Great-Aunt Who Spoke in Italics
—*Onfirethewearygohome*

>　Weakness has no lilt, really. *No fainting*
>　*spells.* No housebroken eclipse. *No wild sighs*
>　*into handkerchiefs.* Their baby sprawled open
>　all plush & nap-fattened: his strength
>　comes through like teeth. *Quietly.* These rooms
>　are asleep, the pipes not speaking, water
>　rests in their elbows. *Silence.* (She pins up
>　her hair— fanatical crown of pentecostal
>　cursive— & wields her unsung tongue
>　over underbite: 30 crooked birds
>　perched in a shut place. They sing only
>　of things too fragile to hold in your pocket.)

A. Loudermilk, Bloomington, Indiana, often writes to remember a (mostly fictionalized) great aunts' and grandmothers' generation of "pocketbook women" in Southern Illinois. Recent honors include: The Second Annual Swan Scythe Press Chapbook Competition, The Phyllis Smart Young Prize in Poetry, and honorable mention in The Randall Jarrell Poetry Competition.

Tribal Bells
7½" x 7½" Black Ash, Pine Needles,
Quills, Bells
by JoAnne Russo

Taylor Graham

Poetry

Tent Caterpillars

Over time I've watched them set up camp
in the neighbor's English walnut:
first, one shimmery pavilion
on an upper branch, and then another.
Moonlight caught a small tent-city
suspended above growing grass;
by mid-July a ghostly network
linking twig to twig. I wished
my neighbor would look to his own
backyard, where elms and maples
stood their distance, watching.
Such gossip in the trees
while I tried to sleep,
and dreamed caterpillar voices
with intent of breaking into wings,
a bureaucracy of bugs listening
to the secrets of leaves,
their flutterings without a wind,
their green assets brittling.

Prehistory

My mother was a dancer at the Isla
Dorada, each evening wrapped up less and less
in what she put on, her morning hopes
diminishing to the point
of spotlit darkness and scant pay.
And afterwards, her single dance
through blinding intersections while,
in the side-ways, safe strangers already
slept, and the night air shook off its scents
of a barely-vanished evening slipping
into so long ago, and shivered a whole city's
wishes into keyholes, and she closed
her doors behind her.

Taylor Graham is a volunteer search-and-rescue dog handler in the Sierra Nevada. Her poems have appeared in *America, The Iowa Review, Poetry International,* and elsewhere. Her latest collection, *An Hour in the Cougar's Grace* (Pudding House, 2000), received a Pipistrelle Best of the Small Press Award.

Featured Artist
Interview by W.A. Reed

Luoyong Wang: The Engineer

Luoyong Wang and W.A. Reed at the Cedarburg Performing Arts Center,
Cedarburg, Wisconsin

Luoyong Wang was born and raised in the People's Republic of China. At age eleven, he began acting training at the Hubei Shi Yan Beijing Opera School. After attending the Wuhan Conservatory of Music to study French Horn, he received a B.A. from the Shanghai Drama Academy and in 1989, his M.F.A. from Boston University's School of Theatre Arts.

As an Assistant Professor (Acting and Stage Movement), Wang has taught for many years at the University of Wisconsin- Milwaukee, and at the Shanghai Theatre Academy. His film and TV credits include *Dragon* (Universal), *Daylight* (Universal), *Concerto of Life* (Beijing Film Studio), *Lana's Rain* (Reigning Pictures, Chicago), *Vanishing Son* (Universal), *Third Watch* (NBC), *New World* (China Central TV), *Lin Ze Xu* (Fujian TV, China), and *The Story of Liaozai* (Shanghai TV). His theatre credits include Seattle Repertory Theatre, L.A. Theatre Center, Shakespeare Festival, Wheelock Theatre (Boston), Milwaukee Chamber Theatre, and Four Sea Players Theatre. He was the first Chinese-American actor cast in the principal role of The Engineer in *Miss Saigon*, which he played for more than five years on Broadway.

Porcupine: You were named after the city in which you were born.

Wang: Close. Luo*yang*. I was born there, in the city *Luoyang*. My grandfather had been classified as a counter-revolutionary and sent to the camp. Once you're classified in that social status, your family pretty much loses all privileges— to schools, good jobs. At a young age, my mother was sent out, away from Shanghai. Shanghai was the most privileged place to be. For her, to leave her home town and be alone was always a source of fear. Later on, she wanted to be reminded that existing in this world means courage. So she changed the last syllable... *yong*, that is the courage.

Porcupine: Describe your childhood.

Wang: My father had a military background... the discipline, to be on time. Very rigid. But my mother's family were considered intellectuals. From them we heard stories about French food, Russian tea. American automobiles. We heard about British literature, philosophers in Germany. So it was a bizarre combination. For years I felt torn. We'd join my grandparents at teatime to drink red tea with brown sugar, read literature. My grandfather would recite in Russian or French or English. I remember as a reward for my success in spelling, he promised to teach me French and English, maybe Spanish.

When my grandfather became a prisoner, he couldn't talk to us. For years. As a young boy in school, I always wanted to be accepted by the group. I was capable of doing anything the other kids could do, but we were being totally rejected. I remember, vividly, during the first days of the Cultural Revolution, these beautiful young and middle-aged women being pushed to the floor and the Red Guard, with the scissors, would cut their pants. They couldn't be too skinny, it was considered the Bourgeois lifestyle. I saw people with a wave in their hair, some naturally born that way, cut on the street. And I heard screaming. A week later, all the engineers, accountants, writers... anyone well-educated or considered intellectual, was lined up with signs that said *spies, imperialist assistants, capitalist supporters. Secret knowledge carriers.* I thought, *wow!* Those big words I didn't even know. Of course then, I learned my

grandfather was in the line, later my mom. And my father— same thing, married to a spy daughter.

Porcupine: At such a young age, was it a source of pride or embarrassment?

Wang: Total embarrassment. Because you were spit on by everyone. I heard people argue on the street, on the bus. In the public parks. But those people were the reddest red. No spies, no foreign relationships. Nobody living abroad. Anyone with an educational background could talk only behind closed doors with the curtains drawn.

By then, my grandfather had been forced into labor camp. In his sixties, he worked ten hours a day digging dirt out of tunnels under Shanghai. One day I brought him his lunch, drink. His teas. He looked me in the eye and said *try to do everything good, this whole thing gonna pass soon. Don't looking at me let you down.* It was funny, somehow. Because at the time I really thought about him with a mixture of hating and mystery, wondering *why don't you just confess?* Once you hear everyone telling you your grandfather's a spy, you say *stubborn old man, why don't you just open your mouth?* I never dared to talk to him like that. Of course I regret now, feeling the way I did. But at the time, I thought my family had done something wrong. I'd lost the faith.

Porcupine: How were you drawn to theatre?

Wang: Escape. It was a way for me to escape.

Porcupine: You were educated at the Hubei Shi Yan Beijing Opera School, then the Shanghai Drama Academy.

Wang: A group of students had been talking about the local Beijing Opera Company looking for youngsters. I said I'd go there. In China, actors were considered the lowest low. Families wanted their kids to go into science or politics or literature. My family told me that good boys never go to the military, never to theatre. Military was dangerous, theatre was prostitution or something. But then I went to audition with them. And I saw those teachers showing all the kids on the dance floor, flipping in the air with their first year students. I thought: *Oh my God. It looks so cool!* And also the beautiful girls and boys were dancing and laughing. I'd never seen open laughing and shouting in school. This was like a paradise for me.

So I went in. They asked me to dance, I couldn't dance. They asked me to sing, I didn't know the song. But I'd taught myself how to play the flute, so I took out my flute and played for them. Out of the thirty or forty kids from my neighborhood, I was the only one who got in. That's the strange thing about being a child in China. One minute you're facing the rice paddies, the next minute you're working in the Beijing Opera School.

Porcupine: And from there, to Shanghai?

Wang: First to Wuhan, the Conservatory of Music. While at the Opera School, I'd get up very early to go out to play my flute. Often I'd see cows in the morning. One day I heard this kind of cow-ish, very dreamy sound coming out of the bamboo forest. I thought: *what is that?* So I went there and found an old man playing French horn in a small

Photo by Vicki Reed

clearing. I asked him what it was and he said *French horn... shhh, don't talk about it. Call it round horn.* He let me try it, then loaned me a mouthpiece. I went home, practiced every day.

During the Cultural Revolution, we had to criticize foreign films. We saw this ballet, black and white film. *Swan Lake*. The moment I heard the round horn, I was mesmerized. I knew I wanted to play it. Later, when I told the old man I'd seen *Swan Lake*, he said *you saw it? I saw it in the fifties!* He gave me five bars and told me *don't practice them together. Hold your long notes.* When Wuhan Conservatory of Music came to audition, I snuck in with my mouthpiece. Someone loaned me a horn and I played for them. They said I was good but because of my background, they'd only let me in as an auditing student. There I studied French horn—until I saw a production of *Hamlet*, and my heart was stolen.

I said *I'm going to become an actor.* At Wuhan, my French horn teacher was grabbing my shirt with all his passion, begging, saying *you'll kill me, Luo, why are you doing this?* He told me I'd regret it, that music was the best, the safest. But I was determined, so I prepared *To be or not to be...* day and night, day and night. The piece is kind of a feeling from my childhood. I walked into the audition the last day, teachers already wrapped up and leaving. I was late because my permission had not been in order. The teachers asked *why you so late? If you're serious, get here early.* I said *listen, I have a Hamlet for you.* They sat back with their arms folded. *Okay, do your Hamlet.* Wuhan is very hot in July. As I started, I saw them scratching, squirming in their seats. Not really paying attention. As I went on, they began to focus, to slowly take notice. I gave them my best Hamlet, even had a tear rolling down my cheek. I was accepted into the program, which was for four years. There, I studied Stanislovsky, Brecht.

Porcupine: How did you happen to come to the United States?

Wang: After I graduated from the Shanghai Academy, they decided to keep me as a teacher. I was the youngest teacher there. I was pissed off because I wanted to be an actor. They said *if you don't want to be a teacher in Shanghai, go to Louisiana— Baton Rouge or somewhere... go to Racine,* someplace like that. I said okay. A couple months later they asked me to go to Belgium to do *Hamlet.* There I met an American delegation (Kristin Linklater) who invited me to Massachusetts.

Porcupine: And to Boston University, in particular?

Wang: Actually, first I did go to Baton Rouge. But they wanted me to make a tape and when they found out I couldn't speak English, they canceled my scholarship. At this time I remembered Kristin Linklater. She invited me to her class. After learning English and playing Romeo *(Romeo and Juliet)* at the workshop, Boston University offered me a scholarship.

Porcupine: You became the first Chinese-American actor to play the principal role in *Miss Saigon.* What did that mean to you in personal terms, and in terms of your career?

Wang: When I finally stood on Broadway... it was

something I had never dared dream about. The enemy I'd been fighting all those years was myself. Believe your family, don't believe your family. Believe in yourself, don't believe in yourself. When I stood there it finally dawned on me: *it doesn't matter how bad you are, how little you know— you can*

have a dream, you can believe your internal voice.
Wanting generates a tremendous energy.

Porcupine: You grew up during the Cultural Revolution, at a time in China when personal freedoms were being rescinded or revoked. I've heard you say once you felt the experience of no censorship in America, that to you it meant you could walk on the moon.

"It is not my job to blame anyone. It is my job to improve my craft. There are two sides to the controversy. (Producer Cameron) Mackintosh should have had more trust in the Asian actors. And the actors should realize that they need to improve their skills."

—Luoyong Wang (on the storm of protest that erupted when Jonathan Pryce was originally cast as the Eurasian Engineer in *Miss Saigon*)

Wang: It was amazing to see, amazing to experience.

Porcupine: Poet Marilyn Chin writes about Chinese-Americans as *the Model Minority*, a term which politicians have used to pit one minority against another.

Wang: Asian culture is heavily influenced by tradition, religion. Confucius teaches us to be respectful of others, particularly our elders. The culture encourages modesty. You meet someone on the street, you assume they know more than you. You see three men together, there must be a teacher— if not for your own field, for something you don't know.

Porcupine: She says she uses the phrase with an edge. That Chinese-Americans are stereotyped as being hardworking, submissive, quiet... almost invisible. That you won't rock the boat.

Wang: Because of the language, and the political situation, many of the stories from China have remained untold. Tiananmen Square was a disappointment to us all. Many Chinese-Americans are stereotyped that way because of their chosen profession. Few Chinese involved themselves in theatre training in 1986. I was always told that to go to Hollywood, you had to be cocky. If you're cocky, you can overpower others, people believe you. To me, that's an insult to others.

Porcupine: She says that although the country is lost, rivers and mountains remain.

Wang: As with any society, modern life sometimes pushes us to where we lose ourselves. But once you open the door and give people a taste, there's no going back. Just give it a little time.

Porcupine: Do you feel disconnected from China?

Wang: When my friends tell me *oh my God, we just heard this great contemporary American musician!* and I ask *who?* and they say *John Denver,* I feel disconnected. People have to travel, to meet people. I want to help them, the same way you'd want to help a homeless man.

Photo by Vicki Reed

Porcupine: Are you in exile?

Wang: I've been warned to be careful. I'm not interested in overthrowing the government, I just want an exchange, a dialogue. When I return to China, even as an actor, I'm still made to feel welcome.

Porcupine: How do you prepare for a role?

Wang: I pull from my own experience. I watch movies,
               read books. I talk to teenagers, or just hang out.
               You can learn a lot from studying teenagers,
               especially if you're preparing for a role you know
               nothing about. I watch people. Even you as you
               spoke with [playwright] Tom Patrick, and your
               mother-in-law. I listen to speech patterns and
               rhythms, watch your movements. It's kind of
               sneaky. If I were a painter or a photographer, I'm
               constantly sketching, taking pictures. The more
               inventory you have, the better equipped you are to
               deal with different situations.

---

*"I remember... my Tai Chi master, who taught me
how to focus— to prepare myself to work. In
Boston, when I was babysitting, the little girl who
would say: 'Luoyong, it's father, not fadder.' I
consider them all to be my teachers."*

—Luoyong Wang (1997)

Porcupine: But performing the same role for years on
               Broadway... how do you stay focused, keep the
               performance fresh and alive?

Wang: I take something away with me, something new,
               each time I play it. There's no set method. Some
               nights, I feel natural. I'm that guy. Other nights, I
               put an ice pack on my neck to provide a sharp
               sensation, to focus me. Or I soak my feet in hot
               water in the sink. I do a hundred pushups or listen
               to New Age, Frank Sinatra. When you go through
               that, you have so many ways— *if this works, I'll
               try it.* As an actor, you cannot become a machine.
               You need to understand how your body works.
               You need the inner dialogue.

Porcupine: Whom do you consider to have been your greatest influence?

Wang: My grandfather. When he was released from prison, he was given an apology and money from the government. By then he was seventy-five years old. First thing, his goal was to translate science books, and documents on logic. He'd refused to translate Karl Marx. He spent fifteen, eighteen hours a day, very little sleep. But by the time I got to Shanghai, he was paralyzed and couldn't talk anymore. He'd had a stroke from a fall he'd taken. My grandfather... he loved a sharp pencil, always wrote so clean.

Porcupine: In 1984 you saw Arthur Miller direct *Death of a Salesman*.

Wang: The end of 1984, yes. The set was great, the fifties music. At that time, I was trained to be sensitive to any type of music. The publicity was huge, all the hype, but I wasn't turned on by the production because I didn't understand about the insurance money.

Porcupine: That was in China?

Wang: Yes.

Photo by Vicki Reed

Porcupine: And in 1985 you performed *Hamlet*.

Wang: Yes, in Paris.

Porcupine: Later, major roles in regional theatres: the title role in *The King and I*, Song Liling in *M. Butterfly*, Lucky in *Waiting for Godot*, and Father's Youth in *The Woman Warrior*.

Wang: I learn something from every performance, every role I play. From every audience. Those performances... *Waiting for Godot* I did in Boston, *The Woman Warrior* at Berkeley Repertory, others at the Chamber Theatre here in Milwaukee... all of them were important in shaping my career. Of course they were. Because English is still my second language.

"I released my experience, my frustration with English. I let it all out there. They all straightened their spines immediately. I saw hope that day, that moment. I sang the whole song of The American Dream. *Then they asked me to sing another song. I sang* Love Me Tender, *and they all cracked up. I knew then I could do it."*

—Luoyong Wang, on using his life experience as material for the *Miss Saigon* role (1997)

Porcupine: Then the audition for *Miss Saigon*.

Wang: I'd come to New York for a short visit. In 1991. A friend of mine told me to see the play, and to look for the Engineer. I was overwhelmed by the production. The whole time I was watching, what I kept hearing in my heart was: *I can do the part of the Engineer. I can do it!*

Porcupine: The Engineer is generally seen as an undesirable character.

Wang: He personifies the sleaziness of Saigon during the Vietnam War. He's a hustler, a swindler. But the Engineer's not completely evil. He's also a survivor, with a fantasy of life in America. He's hopeful, optimistic. The things he does are to stay alive.

There are times during the play, at the end of the first act, when the audience hates him. But they understand him. And in the end I think they sympathize with him.

Porcupine: He's also charismatic... with resiliency, and certain redemptive qualities.

Wang: Sure. Any character is made up of many dimensions.

Porcupine: Don't you feel an audience can despise a character, but at least at some level, to connect with the character, it's important that they care about him?

Wang: That's the job of the writer. And of the actor.

Porcupine: *The New York Times* said not only were you physically right for the part of The Engineer, but that you played it closer to the ground; that you're less a cynical manipulator than a wily street hustler whose desperation to escape Southeast Asia is almost touching. Are you pleased by that characterization?

Wang: Yes, totally. Because I'm not cynical. Acting is the hardest job— four weeks to recreate someone's entire lifetime and make it believable. When I saw Jonathan Pryce play the part, I loved it. But then I thought *maybe he's never been to Asia, maybe he's never seen the labor camps.*

Photo by Vicki Reed

I'm not cynical. Facing some of the people my family considered traitors... I'd hated them for many years. But when I came to understand they were not born bad people, that they reported my grandfather to survive— to save their newborn children, their sons...

Porcupine: Connecting with the audience.

Wang: Yes.

Porcupine: Using your own life experience.

Wang: Whenever I sing *The American Dream*, it reminds me of how I used to think of America while still in China. It reminds me of the dreams and false hopes I had— to read ten thousand books, travel, make a thousand friends. And of all those life experiences.

W.A. Reed, Cedarburg, Wisconsin, is a poet, novelist, engineer, and Managing Editor for *Porcupine Literary Arts Magazine*. His poetry and technical papers have appeared in numerous publications.

CJ Muchhala

Poetry

Peripheral Visions

The wind says bend, the trees bend.
The wind says shake all your yellow hands at once
and the trees comply.

I invented this life. Now I stumble over its roots.

If a bird stops, it sings to me of places I've only guessed at.

A creature shrieks in the night, startles
us from sleep.
The window opens onto moonlight
flat against snow, bright patches
darkening with blood, a shadow spreading
its wings.

CJ Muchhala, Shorewood, Wisconsin, writes: "Most of the clarity we achieve in our lives comes from the periphery of our sight— whether it's the shock of recognizing that we have limited control over our lives, or realizing that final decisions, made early on, no longer fit as we grow into ourselves." Her work has appeared most recently in *The Worcester Review*. New poems are forthcoming in *Wisconsin Academy Review* and *Visions International*.

George Staehle
Poetry

A Little Night Music

When I snore,
my wife dreams I'm a cello
moaning sensuously
on its tanned shellacked back.

Her hand discovers a bow
on the bed stand
instead of the Off button
on the snooze alarm.

She draws the bow back and forth
across the chello's naked belly
and hums Suite Number One
for Unaccompanied Stomach.

A relaxed Mozart aire drifts in
through the bedroom window,
carrying a flutist painted on a potter's
spinning vase, slowing down so fast

that the drowsy notes are stolen
by a clarinet,
then by a tuba,
as I snore deeper.

Stopping by Mom's

Plums huddle in a bowl
on your kitchen table
like red-versus-blue-shirted little boys
piling on a playground football.

A bell drives
their goat-thin legs
to a vanishing point
of brick and arithmetic.

The sun slides down
the schoolhouse roof,
and tall white shirts and business ties
march out in perfect order.

I eat one last memory-sweet plum
as I leave again
and think I see you crouch down
to give your eight-year-old son
the lunch pail and kiss
that send him kicking stones
down maple-tree streets.

Kisses Like Chocolate

When you kiss me goodnight
it's like a chocolate,
gift-wrapped and mint-centered.

Even though
it's my only one of the day
from what I know
is a large box
of chocolates,

that's better
than a box
with no chocolates
and much better
than a chocolate
with no center.

George Staehle lives in the San Francisco-Oakland Bay Area where he has worked for over thirty-five years as a physicist on government defense projects. Before the end of the Cold War, he wrote articles proposing models for cooperative U.S.-Russia projects aimed at gradual disarmament. He is semi-retired and since 1994, has concentrated on poetry.

Stephen R. Roberts

Poetry

Man Believed to be Mad, in the Mood for Soup

A man opens a can of soup.
It is not soup but a flower.
One portion of a plant.
A blossom pouring
from his fingertips.
Part of a garden
he remembers.

Creamy smooth textures
if he stirs the earth
at proper intervals.

Garish hues swirl
in the soiled sky
frantically extracting
the plants to wilt them
under a noonday sun.

Too hot for soup, he thinks.
He opens a can of lemonade.
It is not lemonade.

Green

I notice green this morning.
And the absence of green.
Bird song.
And the spontaneity of silence.

A picnic table and wood pile
each in its own biased grain
displaying the essence of trees.

How flowers reach far beyond themselves.
How trees, if left to themselves,
establish the very edge of the sky.

How the killdeer, on its stone nest,
arranges bits of leaves and litter
for the eggs to know perfection.

I notice blue this morning.
A pristine blue.
Though the eggs are speckled.
And green.

Stephen R. Roberts, Westfield, Indiana, works as an insurance claims adjuster in the cornfield-suburban wilderness of central Indiana. He has had poems recently published in *Cumberland Poetry Review* and *Blue Unicorn*. His most recent chapbook, *Small Fire Speaking in the Rain*, was published by Talent House Press.

Mark Krueger

Fiction

Listening to John Taggart Read *When the Saints* at Woodland Pattern Bookstore (#2): The Art of Paging

I enter. There is a small line, of people, the smell of books.

"Member?"

"Yes."

She, the woman, who works here, gives me a discount. Five bucks. A cheap ticket, for a reading.

I enter a larger room with books and no windows, a room like the basement of City Lights where I paged through Sartre, *The Wall*, I remember, until the doors closed. I browse through several books. Each book, like the readers, different. Some good, some bad, but different, for the most part, than books in big chain stores, not many with windows either.

The books here are musty. They have a shelf life, not like the fresh books in chain stores, hot books that sell, move in and out. I am comfortable here in a room with musty books and no windows. I like to page through books, the paging more pleasing than the reading. I like to think of it as the art of paging. I am in these pages, I tell myself, turning, liberating words.

The lights dim. The reader is about to release words from the page. I've been to several readings here, some good, some bad, but all different. I do not listen to what the words mean, per se. I let them soak in gradually. In hindsight, I find meaning in the movement, like in the paging, of words.

I try not to applaud. I want to be a genuine listener, one

who does not hear what the words mean, until later, with hindsight. Sometimes, I can't help myself. I clap anyway. I tell myself I'm clapping for the liberation of words. But it's not true. I clap because I don't want to be noticed. I want to be an anonymous listener, one who does not draw attention to himself.

I try not to laugh either. I'm not here to be entertained. I'm here to let words soak in. Often, however, I can't help myself. I laugh anyway.

Sometimes my legs ache. They're sore from running. I have to shift position, move sideways to the words. Some words wash past me, because of this change in position. So be it. Every word does not have to be, nor can it be, captured. Plenty will soak in, if I refuse to listen to the meaning, per se. Experience has taught me this. Being here, is enough. "Comfortable," as Simon Ortiz, who was here one night, read, "with the space that is yourself." A reader, reading, my mind free of cant, as Harold Bloom, who has not read here, but who knows a lot about reading, wrote.

Before I discovered how to sit and listen, I was a pretender, a listener of words who did not hear. Now I fashion myself as a true listener, a listener in the poet's audience. The listener, who lets words wash over and through him, some words sinking in later with hindsight.

The owner introduces the reader, John Taggart. A tall, thin, man, rises, slouches over his book, *When The Saints*.

"The problem is..." he begins.

Lost lovers, wit, rhyme, pauses ignored, I write later, sitting with both feet planted on the ground.

"Roses," he says.

Roses? A problem, roses? I ask myself. Thorns, I suppose.

He continues:

"for something to happen

in an enclosed place enclosed space

a room,"

he reads my mind, the thoughts I had earlier in the room without windows. This room, the one in which he is reading, without windows also, I notice, just now, again.

"A space of provocation."

I shift my position so I can face the words fully.

"Words cut by"

I like the sound of that: words cut by. He's a good poet. I need no history of this man. He is his words as they move, liberated from his mouth. Jazz, pure jazz, in the reading of words; precision, man and word, one. He is not a performer, John Taggart. He is a reader of words written to move.

"Hooper" he says.

Edward, I respond. Shadows, light and dark. A naked woman in front of a window. A still life in motion, subject of another Taggart book, on the table, in the other room, which I paged through earlier.

"Air, ashes, burnt roses," the words come quickly now. My legs ache. I shift position. Breathe.

"Charlie Parker."

There it is, of course. He said it, Charlie Parker. Jazz is jazz, what else need be said.

"Minimal harmonic expression."

Yes, that's it, that's what needs to be said. Now for sure, nothing else to be heard. I look at the crowd. Some people are nodding their heads, pretending to get it.

"Rilke."

Just when I thought there was nothing more to be heard, I hear Rilke, which was said before with Hopper, but I did not hear Rilke then, or see, what I see now, the light that entered the caged Panther's eyes. Taggart's eyes, light entering in tribute to his friend, sculptor, Bradford Graves, who has died.

The subject of this book: death. Lest I forget, death. There is a stone sculpture, a xylophone on the cover of the book, which rests on my lap. A book I will read later to liberate the words and to find meaning in hindsight, new meaning amidst the words that drift into the air, "burning, ashes," as the author said or I think he said with precision.

I want to be strong, but *I can't be.* I identify with this poet, his words and movements, his jazz. I can not escape these influences of liberated words leaping from his mouth into thin air and washing over me. Sometimes, not always, this happens at Woodland Pattern bookstore: I am influenced in good and bad ways. Usually I don't know until the words appear on my own pages and even then not until the rereading. But tonight, I sense influences in advance.

I try to shut down, lest I die, suffocate in influences. For a moment, I succeed. My mind wanders, drifts with words out the door. The naked woman in front of the window, who I once told honesty is only part of the truth. What will she think of me with these new influences, a changed man? A man of words, of his own words, influenced by listening without meaning. Here it is, proof in these influences. Just as she is my imaginary audience, I am the genuine audience of poets.

What are the others thinking, these nodders of heads, the non-listeners who surround me. Do they hear the xylophone, lest they forget death. Do they *hear* what the poem is about— jazz and death, a nice combination for a poem, jazz and death. Roses too, are nice. And even better, burnt roses to go with words cut by and lost memory in spaces of provocation.

These are good influences, I tell myself. Let them soak in, be not afraid, of these influences: Rilke, Hopper, Charlie Parker, the pauses, where words drift, or do not exist, in the unspoken lines. One line after another, shifted, reorganized, for sound and effect, just so, as he reads, word and man one, drifting from his mouth into thin air. I hear the xylophone. The stone xylophone, sculpted by his friend, his friend dead now, lest I forget.

not without tone

thank you saying

thank you to the roses more than one....

Good words to end this poem for a friend, to end a reading, as well. Words that linger, hang with the listener who listens without meaning, not the laughers, the nodders of heads, but the listener who listens with hindsight.

The humble man sits down, his words read. The song ended, but the jazz continuing. Much yet to be improvised.

He does not want to sign books, I imagine, but he will. He will do his duty. No one escapes, I have found, totally, even the purest of readers and listeners, from the audience, imaginary or otherwise. As long as there are words, there will be audiences of listeners and readers, some good, some bad. The autograph seekers too, will be here.

I leave. The cool autumn air washes my face. I have always liked this feeling of stepping outside. There are no words here, just the sound of traffic. I get in the car and drive home, West to East, over the bridge toward Lake Michigan, feeling as if I have done something to enlighten myself— an evening of culture at Woodland Pattern. Words collected for later use. Words come by with some pain. I sat for these words, the way a model sits for an artist, on a hard chair, my legs aching. I earned these words, I tell myself.

I enter the house. No one is home. No sounds or bodies, except mine. I climb the stairs to the studio, and put on Yo-Yo Ma and Keith Jarrett cello and piano solos. Two men, solo seekers of truth in music without words: minimal harmonic expression. Sounds waiting for the wordsmiths, the poets, who search for meaning in movement and distort the truth. I am a distorter of truth, I tell myself, influenced now by another distorter of truth, a lonely poet, who is his words. A quiet man seeking something other than truth. Or, truth be known, in another light.

There are too many words, in my head. Influences are running wild. I'm lost again. I pick up the album and look at photos in the moonlight that shines through the skylight. Photos I know by heart and do not need to see, really. I page for the sake of paging, through photos now, the paging soothing. Rilke was a pager. He learned how to see. I will look until I can see, I tell myself, as I page myself to sleep.

Mark Krueger, Shorewood, Wisconsin, is a professor of youth work at the University of Wisconsin- Milwaukee. His textbooks, novels (*Floating* and *In Motion*), and short stories are used in universities and programs for youth in the U.S., Canada, and several other English speaking countries.

Linden Ontjes

Poetry

Five Syllable Count of a Six-Sided Form

Thin plates and needles
    or prisms and stars:
shapes determined by
the pressures of cold.

Motionless: without
    heat, the molecules
adopt manners and
    stop their jostling.

Lower case landscape
bright as snow blindness:
    the relentless white
a curse in reverse.

Only one, set off,
set of   blue tracks to
contradict edict
monochromatic.

Below freezing, sounds
grow louder, change pitch
so that footsteps scrinch
like torn styrofoam.

Could you swear which one
    you saw fall first, last
night, so unique for
    a moment, so white?

The snow underfoot
    understands. Go ahead,
fall back   with your
arms outstretched like wings.

Outside the Entrance of Linens for Less on Hanover Street

A man in a wheelchair pencils portraits of cats for spare change.

Each face anchored with a stone and lined up on the sidewalk
next to a can labeled Thank you. The dim and the dark and
the light gray cats. *Pick your own*, he mumbles. *Pay what you want.*

He's drawing from memory each stray that lives in the city:
their dockyard tails and yardbird eyes, crooked spines and
false designs of tiger stripe or tortoiseshell. He knows them well.

The man in the wheelchair knows how to draw what a cat sees
in the dark. The blurred fur of other cats, the anonymous building
where light turns the corner, the black moon hanging in a white sky.

The one he draws next he will keep for himself. A cat
with nine tails that scales a high-rise, using its retractable
claws, carrying the man in its mouth like a broken bird.

Four Lectures
with Overhead Projector and Pointer

1.
This is a box of sleep
    with tongues.
This is your heart
    packed like a suitcase.
This is the blue
    that means business.
This is a man who lives
    inside November.
These are nine Germans
    shaking their heads.
This is a marcescent hope
    which will never bear fruit.
This is the slow spiral
    of the winged seed.

2.
This is to identify blue
    in a police lineup.
This is the market where
    owners sell their pets.
This is a hand puppet worn
    on the foot.
This is what oxygen means
    when it sets itself on fire.
These are your twin lungs
    pumping like all get out.
This is the one-armed bandit
    which spins lemons
into melons.
This is a thief in the night.

3.

These are the rapid eye movements
      of the guilty, asleep.
This is the blue
      found in the phone book.
This is in praise of the
      minute hand and hour hand
which keep separate
      track of equidistance.
This is to count off
      into squads and climb ropes.
These are the notes mothers
      pin to their children.
This is the dupion hung
      from a mulberry bush.
This is the secret of tarmac.

4.

This is the disguise blue hid
      in the hamper.
This is the corrupt taste of lipstick
      left by her kiss.
This is a hunk of rattlesnake agate:
      Gorilla Playing a Tom-Tom.
This is the truth-function
      of a bowl of plastic fruit.
This is the anger of pronouns.
This is a lecture with overhead
      projector and pointer.
Is this enough to go on?
                  Is this?

Linden Ontjes lives in a log home on the banks of the Tanana River outside Fairbanks, Alaska. She wrote *Five Syllable Count of a Six-Sided Form* after reading about Snowflake Bentley, a Vermont farmer in the early 1900's who spent his life photographing snowflakes. Her poetry has been published in many journals, including *Ploughshares, Prairie Schooner, Nimrod,* and *Exquisite Corpse.*

Thomas David Lisk

Prose Poetry

Sacred and Profane Love

Suddenly the clock felt uneasy in his deerskin ship; exposed beams blue with weary age creaked, but the hull held. Horses in the hold were crazy with terror at the moment the storm cracked and tipped the masts with lightning. A delicate electricity surged through him when you held out your palm full of "borborygmy" and some aboriginal word he was too nervous to "get." Sidling up to desire, red canticles chid his foreboding, and you politely asked for confirmation the j was to be sounded in the artist's name, where it appeared at the very end instead of at the beginning yodeling Jung, or even whispering Jahweh— though whisper Jahweh you did.

Surgery was unnecessary. Your fine veins were all exposed already and he felt portly as an English dinner, his own veins reddening his face, and empty as a balloon, poking his shy nose in your tight-girt business of bliss wisely chosen after a happy struggle with Britannica and World Book. Just around the corner and an hour in the past in the seventies kitchen Mrs. G. Washington stood marshalled, holding a barely-used glass plate speckled with three white crumbs, and an azure napkin with an almost invisible winter red kiss.

Someone he couldn't place assured him she herself was mediocre— or her work anyway— but you were great, brilliant, an amethyst among fire lumps, and (he learned like lightning), on close acquaintance a mounting pleasure to behold. It suddenly occurred to him you might be Elizabeth Vigée-Lebrun living Picasso's life in the Appalachian piedmont, and he wanted immediately to step inside your barbed wire, your electrified fence, and be safe, but you had gone out to the builder's truck to look for a watercolor magazine (the builder's work and yours are not segregated and the magazine might have been in a tool box or on the seat beside a lunch pail); the master builder had, however, emptied the vehicle, so all your interlocutor got to see was your brilliant imagination and you, who penetrated him instantly and filled him with windows and doors you eyed with recognition but refused to stroll through. The picture always captures *was* and *will*, and *is* and *cannot* escape into the outer dark.

You don't drink. Do you eat enough? Is riding Pegasus your primary recreation? Trapped by circumloquacity he couldn't think: handicap, Nootka, squamous, futtock, humble uncle, virgule, hash mark, amblyopia, mono- and dicotyledon, artichoke or argyle, and monkey puzzle tree. You were completely at ease in the looming face of his obvious silent panic. Things you may live without: cotton swabs, talcum powder, salve, Cheetos, a leather bellows, a dog, a god, relics of all kinds, framed oil paintings by artists now dead and forgotten (one has a copper b.b. among the waves where he shot it, half by accident, some time in the past, which is another thing you can live without, especially his). Did you really name your favorite gelding Indigestion, or is equine afflatus a truism?

Some magical wiring pricks him out of safety to define his balloony emptiness against your compact gist radiant with fulfilled identity. Some thing, some force should drive empty rhetoric into the dirt to make it fertile and encourage its rebirth. All the names for art are immortality, safety and control. He too came from pig earth, and when he flips the thin pages it is always the lurching radiance of beauty— however it be trimmed, duplicated and placed— that tears him from the heaving, frightened beast and sheathes him in internal eternal youth.

Thomas David Lisk, Raleigh, North Carolina, is Head of the Department of English at North Carolina State University. In addition to a previous appearance in *Porcupine*, his recent work has appeared in *Arts and Letters, The Literary Review, Boulevard, Painted Bride Quarterly*, and others.

John Parras

Poetry

Bite

The ear is a dried
apricot, slightly
blushed with sunlight.
I could bite
the apricot's soft
wrinkle, suede
child's tongue,
small and oval.

Painful fruit
of summer
I could chew you
out of pure love
tear your soft skin

douse you with ocean
spray the sun
burns away
leaving pinkness
and tears.

Sanded wrinkles
carrying the sea
's salted whispers
I could easily

nip the gentle
crescent's perfect
seashell curve,
diminutive, enraging
ear's lip.

I could clip the lobe's
closed bud, pulpy
raisin of flesh ripe
with its own pristine
seductions.

What distant planet
conceived the pain
of apricots?
What hunger stirs
the tongue to taste
itself? What love
raises its very hand
to slap its own
soft skin?

Palms and fingers
pressing the hot
sand, aching
with summer appetite,
I bite at the heel
and cantaloupe
slice of
the tender instep,
tongue the young
papaya heart
brimming of
wet black seeds.

John Parras, New Milford, New Jersey, studied Creative Writing at Carnegie-Mellon and received his Ph.D. at Columbia. His writings have appeared in *Eureka Literary Magazine, Gulf Stream, Oasis*, and other literary journals.

David Lawrence

Poetry

Brokerage

I suck the aerated plums of negotiated puffery.
It tastes good to get something for nothing, *ex nihilo*.
I serve procrastination
as horse d'oeuvres at business conventions.
There is no opinion like an onion, which cries
at its own sell-out and admits the lackluster surrender
of shaved principals.
I can't keep my head out of its vise
and the veins I pull from my ears are squiggly worms
for bait to migraine suckerfish
who hide their castration in designer suits.
My commission is bare bones.
I throw myself under a train to see if I can keep track.

Auteur

I threw pieces of popcorn at the screen and buttered your lap.
On this occasion of first rate cinema
I discovered that my introspective frame opened
into a ten pound flower.
My panorama is so wide that out-of-synch logic does not hurt me.
Sometimes I wish I were a double feature
and that I shuffled between obstinate choices like a turning point.
I am taking pictures of myself with 35-millimeter film
so I can win an Academy Award in your understanding.
I put nine dollars and fifty cents in my pocket and watch myself roll.

Hugs Cooperate

When we went swimming in the naked mountain lake above dispensation,
we weren't really there but I was imagining your long draft
squeezing the ripples from the water and your cool lips
slipping like a tray of ice cubes.
There were so many things that never happened that are real
and the clock ticking is a pendulum that flicks like a tongue.
In the center of burnt toast the butter slid down the knife
like nostalgia for stale investigations and commensurate blague.
I loved the queen of hearts among all the other playing cards, flipped.
On your lap I used to build sand castles to teach your groin
lessons about the beach falling on redundant horns.
I am startled by the beach ball's notes
and the music of crabs swishing through the undertow like saliva.
Where are we going when the fist fight of the future
has rejected our compromise?
I want to stay with you for as long as an invitation.
I cannot put aside the interminable friction of naïve smooches
and the way hugs cooperate with your appeal.

David Lawrence, New York, New York, is a poet, actor, screenwriter, model, business mogul, boxer, rapper, jailbird, professor, stand-up comic, husband, father, and amiable neurotic. He has been interviewed on CBS, ABC, MSG, BBC, etc., as well as in *New York Magazine, Men's Journal, People Magazine,* and *Sport's Illustrated*. "All for boxing and rapping, not poetry. Not my fault. What does *People Magazine* know about poetry?"

Kenneth Pobo

Poetry

Vern Barningham

A lighthouse keeper,
he timed the lights
to ensure a turning lens—

skippers told islands apart
by his precision,
his constant polish. Some
people would ask did he
get lonely? Four families

who lived away from pigeons
that kept time to city lights
had to get along or anger
cut deep as winter wind. Up
in the lighthouse, silent,

he watched lakebirds, clouds
seizing a skyhook, then
slipping off onto tips
of wave. Many keepers came
to prefer the slap

of water against shore,
seasons like four strange
voices in trees. Storms
couldn't crawl over the light
enough to cover it. Vern

made light the way
farmers coax earth
into harvest.

The Manistee

1883. For five days
we hoped the storm that chained
us to Bayfield would free us.
Lake Superior, a man

dancing alone— he knows
every move, yet who could guess
his calm for killing? Sun out,
we departed, but with this lake's

iron hooks, we risked. Water
had no use for us, grew higher
and wider as we went farther
out, beyond the light,

where land was what we remembered
like childhood. And other life,
unwritten letters and ruptured
promises. When the ship cracked

open, we had no one
to call, no rescue. Wind
carried no messages
and freezing water made short

work of souls. Our bodies
were never recovered. Once
our names sank with the wreck,
our families built absence

a home. In 1884,
fishermen found a silver spoon
engraved with "Manistee"
in a trout's belly.

Kenneth Pobo, Folsom, Pennsylvania, has published work in *American Writing, Orbis, Illinois Review, Spoon River Quarterly*, and others. His 1998 chapbook, *Cicadas in the Apple Tree*, was named a winner of the Palanquin Press Chapbook Contest.

Zan Gay

Poetry

Catfish

The long hours between meals at the VFW home
my father spends reading, most markedly Time
Magazine on Tuesdays, a habit unbroken since 1935.
He triumphs when he finds a mistake
a prestigious New York editor overlooks:
"The sabal palm of Florida isn't spelled *sable*."
He waits for a reply, and soon by formal letter
an attentive executive apologizes and praises
him for bringing the error to light.

Once in awhile my father sends me an envelope,
empty but for an obituary of someone back home
he thinks I know, but don't, or a Time letter.
This latest pertains to a catfish tortured
by a Hudson River otter biting off scales
on one side, making the fish swim in circles.
"Catfish don't have scales," he wrote to Time.
The punctual response from the editorial office
commends my father on his keen eye, "You are right.
The only time catfish and scales should be thought of
together is when you're weighting your catch."

I box the letter with all the others from my father,
this man who deems to be always right
and sends me proof without sweet salutations,
or what I want most, the "Love, Dad."

Growing up we ate catfish when there was nothing else
for the table, the butchering month a half year away,
my brothers sent off to a nearby pond, bringing back

a string of black silurid bullheads and tossing them
under the spigot for my father to clean.
He sliced off their fat heads, careful not to let
the barbels sting him, gutted them and then took
pliers to rip the thick skin down the filets.

My father and I ate only the onions and bread
at supper, the swamp-stink too pervasive
from my brothers' boots for me, and he fearing
fish bones might catch in his throat.

Zan Gay, Coral Springs, Florida, grew up in a post-War Yankee Polish family in 1950's rural Florida, misfits in the deep South. Work is published in or forthcoming from *Feminist Studies, Karamu, Phoebe, Slant,* and *The Louisville Review.*

Jeremy James George
    Poetry

Salmon Cannery, 1991

That summer in '91 I left school in June
and went north to Alaska to flesh-off fish,
to cut short the salmon in their quicksilver

tracks. Each morning I woke, replaced the
blindfold with glasses, walked to the cafeteria
hoping the fish in my dreams would not

be breakfast: I remember coffee, pancakes,
eggs hard-boiled or scrambled, bacon.
I remember riddles and getting stoned to make

the days match the nights, to make the weeks
slide through the months, all games for the sake
of time. Everything from that summer intrudes.

When my girlfriend sent the fifth of Jim Beam
I drank it on the beach in a light fog with friends
from the slime line, both saving and ruining them.

To go backward in time I find the wide album full
of black and white photographs: the airstrip,
the dock, the sunset over the mountains across

the bay— and color photos: a group of haggard men
standing in a Russian church, an aggregate of fish
heading down a conveyor belt. It's true, I might have

pulled all the roe one Japanese man ate that next winter,
scooping the bulbous sacs as if they were gold.
Hold on, I thought then, there is something at the end

of the line, something that says there's a chance
we'll make it through with all our fingers intact.
I didn't see the salmon in the sea that summer.

I watched them come cold and dead from out of an
aluminum chute, lined them up belly to back, watched them
beheaded, definned, gutted and sent to the slimeline like limp

bags of flesh, some scars scraped off, then up the conveyor
to be ground— flesh and bones, scars and muscle—
everything canned, the cans boxed, the boxes put on pallets,

the pallets put on ships, the ships shipped across oceans
where everything reverses, the crates unloaded, singular
cans bought, brought home, opened, eaten, fingers licked.

Things That Live

I sit before a candle reading Rexroth's
"The Signature of All Things." Everyone
is sleeping or simply elsewhere. I go down
close enough to the flame to feel the yellow
on my forehead. It's an hour past midnight
in August in a summer that saw everything come late—
all the color of lupine and fireweed, all
the pink salmon and alder leaf. The flame-
light beckons a shadow and a reflection and
in the silence I listen for something wise,
but nothing obvious comes.

The truth is I don't want to see a bear
unless, speaking to me, the direct tongue
of God cuts through the kitchen darkness
right to where I can see him, hear him.
I'd settle for anything hitched with eloquence,
—a moth, the cat, anything with a sign— anything
with that "electrolysis of love."

High tide now. A single cabin light across
the passage goes faint. The moon-flicker
diminishes between clouds— the world
is closing down. Something invisible and
kinetic sets in: All around are things that live.
The candle flame flutters and fails.
I point to nothing in particular
but on the end of my finger
settles a rich current of stars.

—Kodiak, Alaska

Jeremy James George grew up in Milwaukee, Wisconsin, and has been living in Alaska for four years. He currently works as a long-term substitute teacher in Barrow, Alaska.

Jennifer Dick

Poetry

She Opens Her Mouth to Say

there is only the word, the
hesitation
       like when
he holds her, grabs. mitts of
black tar, red tongue
leering. gaze uninvited, even that
an infraction.
       her hands caught
in a cat's cradle, some barrier,
as when she shuts
the door, leaves the key, there,
so he must knock.
      basilic
wilting on the barred sill
his voice at his own door
pleading. there is no way out
but forwards. his soft hands,
her avoiding,
      as if
even in that, were hidden
the giant lotus blooming between lily leaves
in the botanical garden. some foreign key
only she has seen.
      trembling
at the other side of the door,
a sort of peck-peck-tapping
as of a bird who knows
a meal lies just beyond
the pane it's reaching
through.

Jennifer Dick is currently one of WICE's writers-in-residence in Paris where she teaches English and Creative Writing and co-edits *Upstairs at Duroc*. She has poems published in or forthcoming from numerous journals including *The Portland Review, Whiskey Island Magazine,* and *Frank International*.

Carol Hamilton

Poetry

Deliverance

A river song on the radio
skips after me on a dash
down the highway, slashing
my way home between fields
of feathery green tossed
by evening slant-light
and dotted with cattle
oblivious to the beauty,
I suppose, grinding on
at the emerald grass.
Some are Charolais. Then
the water of the Verdigris
plunges past time and space,
soothes me again from that
pecan grove with my still
young family and friends.
That long-ago day comes
intact with its dreamy fog,
the pale-faced cattle staring
at our cooking fire like
ghosts of the saints hovering
about our doings, curious,
perhaps approving.
The dew-etched spider webs
still sparkle, so tiny
between blades of grass
as we crawl scooping up pecans.
My brain says he was there that day,
but I only remember the rest of us,
the happy circle with conveyer belts

humming, pecans cracking open,
us wrapped in damp white clouds.
That package of honeyed memory
is a time machine, and I rewind it
on high speed, would stand
there and here at once.
The Verdigris meanders on
to New Orleans. It has never
taken me that far. But it has
often dropped this precious cargo
in my hands. Its ways are swift
and selective, and I thank it.

Carol Hamilton was named Oklahoma's Poet Laureate in 1995. She won the *Chiron Review* Chapbook Award 2000 and this year's David Ray Poetry Award from *Potpourri*. Recent and upcoming publications include *River King, Midwest Quarterly Review, Spoon River Poetry Review,* and *Skylark*.

Antler
Poetry

Horizontal Icicles

Just after waking
Look out my window
At horizontal icicles
   on birch branch
Creation of last night
   west wind
         cold snap
So slow drip
   snow melt
Blown parallel to earth
Solidified lengthened thickened
   slowly
         as I slept
   to become
Six six-inch horizontal icicles
Like silver carrots tapering to a point
   each point with a frozen drop
         at the tip
   a few bubbles inside each,
         strange, how?
Striations of color
   making me wonder
         comparison
   cross-section tree trunk
         to cross-section icicle.
My day goes by
   and then it's night
         and I lie in bed
Thinking of stalactites and stalagmites
   long-lived icicles of minerals

in undiscovered labyrinths
in undiscovered caves
Compared to horizontal icicles
in the full moon.

Looking Up at the Milky Way Thought

What must it be like for fish
watching ice form
on the surface of their lake
Or looking up at fish
frozen in ice above them
and feeling the water
Thickening around them
till they too
can't move
But are still alive
looking up seeing
falling snow
Slowly cover the ice
till darkness
engulfs their realm
A poet on his back on snow-covered ice
looking up at the Milky Way
thought.

Antler, Milwaukee, Wisconsin, is the author of *Factory* (City Lights), *Last Words* (Ballantine), *Selected Poems* (Soft Skull), and *Ever-Expanding Wilderness* (forthcoming). His poems have appeared in many anthologies including *American Poets Say Goodbye to the 20th Century, Wild Song: Poems from Wilderness Magazine,* and *Stubborn Light: The Best of the Sun.*

Virgil Suárez

Essay

Bombardment

When I close my eyes, I see the ropes.

Ropes hanging from the paneled ceiling. Ropes and their round metal necks to signify to the climber this is the limit, as far as you can go. This is a gym in Henry T. Gage Junior High School in Los Angeles, California. This is circa 1974.

When I close my eyes I see the braided mesh wire between the glass panes high up on the gym windows where ash and sepia-colored pigeons flock to roost.

When I close my eyes I see the crow, there to steal another pigeon's egg, breaking it open between its own claws, tasting the yoke, looking down at us.

It squawks twice, then takes off with the broken egg in clenched claws.

When I close my eyes I see each letter in the word *bombardment* fall from the rafters down to the bleachers. A bee's buzz around the basketball score-keeper. The "o" of our mouths when Mr. Stupen barks at us to pick teams, knowing how it is going to go.

Lil' Ruben and Ratboy Marcos choose their own team of homeboys-they, of course, are to be *shirts*, though they sometimes wanted to be "skins" to show off their Virgen of Guadalupe tattoos on their pectorals, shoulders or arms.

When I close my eyes I hear the "m" stutter of Benny who always plays on our team, the skins, *los carneritos*, as they call us for *carne*, and he goes down first. Last time he went to the clinic with a bruised rib that hurt like a motherfucker. He believes that once a rib breaks you have less luck in life. Maybe so, Benny. Maybe so.

One time, Chempo, the meanest of them all, got his nose broken. "B" is for ball. Bad ball. For its heavy, dark weight that bruises the skin where the ball makes contact with our bodies.

"A" is for the assholes who gang up against us, allowed to do so by the lack of supervision by the fucked-up gym teachers. Mr. Stupen, bless his masochist heart, never once looked in on us after he blew his whistle to signal the beginning of the 50 minute bout.

"May the last man standing win," he'd say, turn around, and leave for a smoke or a nap, or, rumor had it, spy on the girls in the locker room through a peep hole in his office.

When I close my eyes I see the "R" of his referee, striped shirt.

Stinky Watson, the only white kid on the team, likes to spit loogies into our faces. He spits them like bullets. After each spit, he works the mouth and tongue, saving up some more saliva.

"M" is for *mierda*, for what I always said when I found two or three of Watson's spits in my hair. Though I never liked to shower at school, I would have to. I hated it, the sound Watson made as he hocked up another one.

When I close my eyes I see the entanglements of flesh, how one boy falls on the ground and then there'd be a pile-up. Who didn't believe in the story of Humpty Dumpty, the little egg that fell off the fence and fell apart? You could almost hear the extinction of breath from the victim.

All of us moved back at the start of the game. If there were rules, they were not followed as the homeboys ganged up against us, one by one, drawing us away from the walls to the center of the court where they could take better aim with the bombardment ball and nail us on our backs.

"T" is for the hollow *thuck-thuck* of that ball hitting our flesh.

"*Pinches cabrones,*" Ramirez, the Mexican, would say. He was made crazy at school by bombardment.

When he and his family crossed the Rio Grande, bombardment wasn't the school activity he had in mind. He said he'd much rather work in the factories, and he did. A year after they broke his arm, he left school. We never heard from or saw Ramirez again. We need you now, Ramirez. Where are you?

There are three Cubans on the "skins" team and we bonded. We fight back. I stop fighting after they take me down one day and tie me up with the climbing ropes. I believe they will hang me. And if they hang me, I will not ever have to do this again. And they hang me alright, but all they do is line up and throw the ball at my body as hard as they can.

I hang there and they taunt me. A couple miss, and most of the blows come down below the waist. I cover my groin and my head as I try to guess which way the ball is coming at me.

Fifty minutes lasts an eternity. I can hear the sound of my own heart beating between my burning ears. If there is blood coursing through my veins, it is like the Almendares of my childhood in Cuba gushing after a downpour.

When that bell rings, Mr. Stupen never even bothers to come back and blow the whistle, so the gangsters run at us, stampede us with their kicks, wild-thrown punches. They snap their moist-with-sweat, stinky shirts at us.

They claw and tear through our shirts, ripping them off our waists, taking the good ones and keeping them.

Thank God we didn't share lockers with any of them. Us, the recent-arrivals from Cuba, Mexico (Tijuana), Salvador, Nicaragua...we're all wetbacks. Nobody wants us for locker partners. Shit, that's what they call us. The skin shits.

"Wetback skins," someone shouts and then there are the whistles to signify the bomb-ball's drop.

This is warfare. A ball rains down from the I-beam rafters. The *thuds* of the ball hitting our bodies echoes ad infinitum, loud enough to see the pigeons, sparrows, crows aflutter. They are our only audience. Our only witness. I say they are the choir in some Greek drama.

When I close my eyes I see the heavy ball falling from the sky.

"*Wachale!*" someone shouts. "Take cover!"

In my nightmares there's more than one ball. They rain down upon us, knocking us to the ground, breaking our bones.

Nobody ever speaks about this.

We hide our bruised limbs as best we could. From our families. From our parents. "What's that?" my father will say looking at a bruise on my arm peeking through my t-shirt sleeve. "Nothing," I say.

Most of us are twelve, thirteen, fourteen-we don't have to show our bodies to anyone. "Why are you limping?" my mother wants to know. "Shoes," I tell her. "A little tight."

The bruises bloom and darken our skins, spilled ink in water, a flowering right underneath our epidermis where the hurt sends shock-waves to our brain, our hearts.

When we close our eyes we see our broken souls.

When we close our eyes we see the scoreboard and how much we are behind, how much we are losing, how much harder we have to try to keep from going down for good.

When we close our eyes we see nothing but the purple and yellow of our cowardice. How, though we keep getting up and dusting our hands off, we keep getting pushed down, ground by a stranger's heel, our cheeks to the hard earth, our ears tuned to the muted sound of some poor sap somewhere moaning about a nosebleed, a broken finger, a fistful of hair missing.

Thuck-thud, thuck-thud, when we close our eyes we can still hear the most frightening of sounds: a bombardment ball rolling across an empty gymnasium court floor, coming to a final rest under put-away bleachers.

We hear ourselves crying, "stay close, stay together, stay..."

What is the sound of such a big ball whizzing by you, thrown with deliberate speed, with deliberate maliciousness?

What is the sound of that ball, that ball, hitting your rib cage, knocking the wind out of you? Or hitting the back of your head and knocking you down and out, teeth ground into the wood of the floor?

How does your blood taste as you tilt your head up to keep it from trickling down your mouth and chin? It's blood-in-the-water mentality-one drop and they see your weakness. They'll set upon you and beat you to a pulp.

You don't want to let them know your hurt, your pains and aches, the throbbing between your ears. It's a matter of time, you think. It's only a matter of time before something happens and all this fades away.

Nowhere to run, or hide. Stand up straight. Find out your next move.

Move!

Now keep your eyes closed to pretend this heavy, scuffed ball is never going to find you.

Virgil Suárez, Tallahassee, Florida, writes: "Bombardment is part of a book of personal essays I am currently working on, titled *In the Hieroglyphics Garden.*" He teaches Creative Writing and Latino/a and Carribbean Literature at Florida State University. He was born in Havana, Cuba in 1962, and is the author of four published novels: *Latin Jazz, The Cutter, Havana Thursdays,* and *Going Under.*

John Grey

Poetry

The Mourners

You know how it is. So many contacts
with the way things die, we grow immune
to the extinction. A light switches
off. A telephone clicks. A door quietly
closes. We're all our lives being
temporarily cut off from people
yet only when they're really dead
do we make a big show of it.

I promise myself though I'm going to
mourn every chance I get. I'm going
to sob at twilight. I'm turning
ashen when people show their backs. You
say goodbye and I send flowers. I finish
reading your letter and before going
back to the beginning, I have an
entire funeral then and there
around the floral borders of each page.

What's the point, I'm thinking, of
letting it all gush out on dead ground.
May as well let my tears flood a rock
or driftwood on a beach. May as well
proclaim God, I miss that toenail
clipping, that shard of glass.

From now on, whatever is part of me
has to answer for its absence.
Temporary dislocations must be treated
as finalities. Besides, I've always
admired the way people kneel and pray,
weep and remember. For them, it's never again.
For me, it has to be until the next time.

The Last Years of Paganism

The fear of any kind
is not in you.
No current in your modern blood
to circulate my old terrors.
I am the tombstones
in your county graveyard,
the heavy brown
funeral parlor curtains
that dampened your last tears.
You surround me
with the trappings of death,
anywhere the dark can fester.

You reduce me to manageable size
but your curious hands do not
linger around my body,
but grip the implied catafalque
beneath these bones,
your slight frame no indication
of your strength.
You want to be there
at my disintegration,
when the heavy rosewood lid
sets like the ultimate sun,
buries my last horizon.

No longer deified,
I am just a monster
with three heads and bodies
joined at the waist,
some crass Olympian
suffocating in
the Stygian poppies.
My melancholy mausoleum

could gather dust on your shelf,
burn on the willing pyre
of your next cigarette,
be severed at the root
by the turning of your head
towards the next new thing.

John Grey, Providence, Rhode Island, has had work in *Whetstone, South Carolina Review* and *English Journal*.

Kathryn J. Gahl
Poetry

Afterward in Two Rivers

Afterward used to mean pushing back
a chair at the dinner table,
for conversation, a cigar or maybe

it meant the spent look on your face
when you were still inside me,
freed into sweet belly breathing.

Or recall the best afterward at
the bottom of Suicide Hill, after
my sled went faster and farther

than anyone else and my squeal
held in heavens above. But now,
dare it mean apple-red cheeks

after we labor to fill bushels with
Macintosh, Golden Delicious,
and pride before F-16's rumble

overhead to protect the nuclear
power plant not that many
miles from where, afterward,

wild turkeys and their babies
step though tall grasses,
gracious, cautious.

Kathryn Gahl, Two Rivers, Wisconsin, writes short stories, poetry, and children's picture books. Her poetry appears in lieu of liner notes on *Sweet Mango,* a jazz CD. She is currently at work on a novel. This poem came to her while walking her long gravel driveway.

Porcupine #1
10" x 11", Black
Ash, Pine Needles,
Porcupine Quills

Page 31

Cactus
6", Black Ash,
Pine Needles,
Cactus Spines

Page 41

Porcupine-cone #2
10" x 12", Black
Ash, Pine Needles,
Porcupine Quills

Page 45

Onion Dome
10" x 7", Black Ash,
Pine Needles

Page 67

Tribal Bells
7½" x 7½", Black
Ash, Pine Needles,
Beads, Quills, Bells

Page 71

JoAnne Russo weaves very detailed intricate baskets that are inspired by Native Americans of the Northeast and the Southwest. JoAnne mentored with Raymond Weare, the last to learn from the Mount Agamenticus basket makers of Maine, an entire community in the area of York, Maine that once made their livelihood from basket making. From Weare, JoAnne learned to harvest ash trees and pound the growth rings off the tree in order to make the basket splints for weaving— a process that can take weeks. She uses materials taken from the forest: black ash, pine needles, sweet grass and Porcupine quills. JoAnne incorporates strong visual design elements, like the contrast of black and white or spiky surface decorations, to give each basket a presence- an animism.

JoAnne lives in Saxtons River, Vermont.

Russo's baskets often incorporate a variation of a traditional American Indian basket making technique know as "porcupine curlicues." The porcupine curlicue is created by weaving a piece of thin satin ash over an existing row. This second piece is twisted forward and back, which turns it into a point.

Tribal Bells (and/or Onion Dome) incorporates the technique of weaving over a mold that allows the weaver to be in control of the form. The molds that Jo Anne designs and uses are puzzle molds, consisting of nine pieces of wood that fit together perfectly to create the mold shape. Puzzle molds are used for basket shapes where the diameter of the top of the basket is narrower than the diameter of the body of the basket. When the weaving of the basket is completed, the middle piece of the mold can be removed allowing the rest of the pieces to be removed.

Submission Guidelines

Porcupine is published twice each year. Issues contain a mixture of poetry, short fiction, essays, feature interviews, and visual art work. Cover art is occasionally selected from submitted material. We welcome unsolicited manuscripts and art work throughout the year. There are no restrictions as to theme or style. Prose should be readable, professional, and of a high quality. Make us care about the characters. Poetry should be accessible and highly selective. If a submission is not timely for one issue, it will be considered for another.

Send a sampling of visual art work, one prose piece, or one to three poems at a time (mail genres separately). Art work should be submitted as transparencies or 8x10 glossy prints. We can accommodate a limited number of full color reproductions. Black and white is encouraged. Prose should be double spaced on one side only and should be no longer than twenty-five pages (shorter pieces will receive stronger consideration). Although we are interested primarily in short stories, novel excerpts are acceptable if self-contained. Poems should be individually typed on one side of the page. Each page should include the author's name. Feature interviews are commissioned and are not accepted without prior arrangement. Previously published material or simultaneous submissions are not considered.

It is recommended that the magazine be reviewed prior to submitting material (send $5.00 for a sample copy). Submissions should be mailed with SASE to: Porcupine, PO Box 259, Cedarburg, WI 53012. The outside of the envelope should state: "Fiction," "Essay," "Poetry," or "Art Work." Unsolicited material sent directly to an editor's home or office will be discarded. Expect ten to twelve weeks for a response. Payment is one copy upon publication.

Back Issues Available

$5.00 including shipping within USA

Volume 1 Issue 1

Cover Art: Polly Ewens
Interviews: *Peggy Hong* by Amy Franklin,
             Thomas Kubala by Howard Hinterthuer,
             Guillermo Menocal by Jeanette Hurt
Essay: Barbara Joosse
Fiction: Carol Lynn Schowalter, Christine Tachick
Poetry: Judith M. Ford, Hilary Goldblatt, Greg Grummer, Thea
             Kovac, Julie Parson-Nesbitt, Kenneth Pobo, W.A. Reed,
             Robert Siegel, Debra Kay Vest
Portfolio: Photographs of Maine by Vicki Reed
Visual Arts: Sally Duback, Doug Edmunds, Polly Ewens, Thomas
             Kubala, Sarah McEneany, Carri M. Skoczek, Vicki Reed

Volume 1 Issue 2

Cover Art: Vicki Reed and Robert Reddy
Interviews: *Thomas Hoffman* by Mona Bernstein,
             Tony Finlayson by Peggy Hong,
             Martin Jack Rosenblum by W.A. Reed
Fiction: Mary Ann Cain, Dennis Must, Philip Russel
Poetry: Amy E. De Jarlais, Susan Firer, Kimiko Hahn, Kristin
             Herbert, Karen Haas-Howland, Thor Ringler, Joseph
             Rubano, Cheryl Whitehead
Portfolio: Photographs by Doug Edmunds
Visual Arts: Mona Bernstein, Doug Edmunds, Susan Falkman,
             Thomas Hoffman, Leo Pilak, Vicki Reed

Volume 2 Issue 1

Cover Art: *Five Red Horses With Lilies* by Katye Rueth
Interviews: *Jean Crane* by Loretta Strehlow,
             Brana Kevich by Barbara Joosse,
             Charles Radtke by W.A. Reed
Fiction: Thomas David Lisk, Matthew Roberson,
             J.L. Schneider, Carol Lynn Schowalter
Poetry: Jacqueline Berger, Ann Hostetler, Martha Kranzthor-
             Osvat, E.O. Lipchik, Helen Robertson, Loretta Strehlow,
             T.N. Turner
Portfolio: Paintings by Katye Rueth
Visual Arts: Jean Crane, Doug Edmunds, Brana Kevich, Charles
             Radtke, Vicki Reed, Katye Rueth

77

Volume 2 Issue 2
Cover Art: David Lenz
Interviews: *David Lenz* by W.A Reed,
R.J.Siegel by Howard Hinterthuer,
Teri Wagner by Karen Haas-Howland
Fiction: Melodie Starkey
Poetry: Susanne R. Bowers, Bill Embly, Leon De Greiff/(Guevara),
John Grey, Elizabeth Ann James,
B.Z. Niditch, Ilana Simons
Portfolio: Sculpture by Truman Lowe
Visual Arts: Doug Edmunds, David Lenz, Truman Lowe,
Vicki Reed, Teri Wagner

Volume 3 Issue 1
Cover Art: *Goat Boys* by Betty LaDuke
Interviews: *Mireille Favarel* by Mark Cebulski,
Betty LaDuke by Barbara Joosse,
Stanislav Venglevski by W.A. Reed
Fiction: Karen Sharp, Martha Highers
Poetry: Holly Day, Barbara DeCesare, Christine Delea,
Paul J. Enea, Sarah Fox, Andrew Genn-Dorian,
John Grey, B.Z. Niditch, Simon Perchik, Kenneth Pobo,
G.K. Wuori
Portfolio: Photographs of Africa by Vicki Reed
Visual Arts: Betty LaDuke, Vicki Reed

Volume 3 Issue 2
Cover Art: *Lily and Sunflower*, Polaroid transfers by
Sarah McEneany
Interviews: *Joel Pfeiffer* by Barbara Joosse,
Jon Van Zyle by Howard Hinterthuer
Fiction: Paul Lewellan, Terri Brown-Davidson, C.J. Muchhala, Ian
MacMillan, Lydia Webster
Poetry: Arlene Ang, Taylor Graham, Meghan Hickey,
Katherine Holmes, Joan Payne Kincaid, B.Z. Niditch,
Jim Redmond, Todd Evan Temkin, Laurie Ann Whitt
Portfolio: Photographs by Sarah McEneany
Visual Arts: Doug Edmunds, Joel Pfeiffer,
Sarah McEneany, Jon Van Zyle

Volume 5 Issue 2

To Order Single Issues or Subscriptions

Return this form with a check or money order to:
Porcupine, P.O. Box 259, Cedarburg, WI 53012

Name _____

(please print)

Street Address _____

City, State, Zip _____

Yes, I'm subscribing to Porcupine:

☐ **One Year** ($15.95 for two Issues)

☐ **Two Years** ($30.95 for four Issues)

Begin my subscription with: Volume_____ Issue_____

Enter a gift subscription for:

Name _____

(please print)

Street Address _____

City, State, Zip _____

☐ **One Year** ($15.95 for two Issues)

☐ **Two Years** ($30.95 for four Issues)

Begin my subscription with: Volume_____ Issue_____

Sign gift card: _____

(Write additional gift subscriptions on a separate piece of paper)

I wish to order the following single copies:

__Vol. 1, Issue 1   __Vol. 2, Issue 1   __Vol. 3, Issue 1   __Vol. 4, Issue 1   __Vol. 5, Issue 1

__Vol. 1, Issue 2   __Vol. 2, Issue 2   __Vol. 3, Issue 2   __Vol. 4, Issue 2   __Vol. 5, Issue 2

Number of single copies ordered   _____ x **$5.00 =**   _____

Number of One Year Subscriptions _____ x **$15.95 =**   _____

Number of Two Year Subscriptions _____ x **$30.95 =**   _____

Total Amount Enclosed   _____

We Support
the Arts...

Because each artist works to share with us
a spark of creativity that just might ignite
our own dreams.

Carroll Law Office, S.C.

Serving the legal needs of Ozaukee County since 1977;
specializing in real estate, estate planning, and business law.
W62N562 Washington Ave. , Cedarburg, WI 53012
Ph: (262) 375-9800 Fax: (262) 375-9826

Cedarburg Cultural Center

Featuring exhibits that explore the community's history,
heritage and contemporary culture. Open Tuesday through
Saturday 10-5 and Sunday 1-5. Free Admission
W62 N546 Washington Ave., Cedarburg, WI 53012
(262) 375-3676

Cedarburg Floral Studio

Outstanding Flowers, Plants and Design — Guaranteed.
Award Winning Staff, Brilliant Wedding and Sympathy Creations.
Daily Deliveries —1Block East of Washington Ave
W63 N541 Hanover Ave., Cedarburg, WI 53012
(262) 377-0777

John Red's LTD.

"A collection of Amazing Things"
An American Craft Gallery. Representing over 250
American Artists and Craftsmen.
N70 W6340 Bridge Rd. Cedarburg, WI 53012
(262) 377-2995 p/f
www.cedarcreeksettlement.com/JohnReds.html

The Kubala Washatko Architects, Inc.
Dedicated to creating environments for quality
living and working
W61N617 Mequon Ave., Cedarburg, WI 53012
(262) 377-6039 Fax (262) 377-2954

Larry's Brown Deer Market
Specialty Foods, Deli, Take-Out Lunches & Entrees,
Corporate & Personal Catering & Gifts For All Occasions!
8737 N. Deerwood Drive, Milwaukee, WI 53209
(414) 355-9650

Law Offices of Dale & Pakenas
Specializing in cases of serious personal injury and death.
641 W Lake St., Suite 400
Chicago, IL 60661
(312) 258-1800

Reddy & Associates
Graphic design services for businesses and institutions—
giving form to insights.
P.O. Box 639, Cedarburg, WI 53012
(262) 377-8448

U-Line Corporation
Pioneers in Refrigeration
8900 N.55th St., Milwaukee, WI 53223
(414) 354-0300 Email: u-line@execpc.com
Web Site: www.u-line.com

Washington House Inn
A country Victorian inn located in the heart of Cedarburg.
W62 N573 Washington Avenue, Cedarburg, WI 53012
(262) 375-3550 Outside Wisconsin: (800) 554-4717
Gift Certificates available
Web Site: www.washingtonhouseinn.com

SHARP READING

Enjoy every issue of Porcupine Literary Arts Magazine.

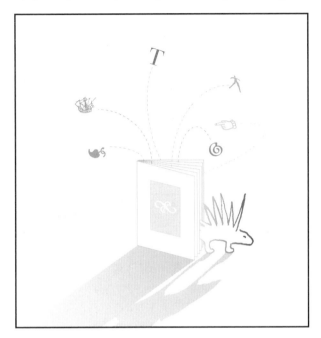

Subscribe today.

Twice a year, a group of dedicated Wisconsin artists create
an engaging compilation of poetry, prose, visual arts and
interviews. Be sure you don't miss a single issue. Each is perfect
bound, with approximately 150 pages, and includes full-color
covers and black & white contents. Spring/Summer &
Fall/Winter issues. Subscribe today.

Please indicate which subscription length you prefer:
1-year subscription (two issues) is $15.95.
You save $1.95 over the regular single copy price.
2-year subscription (four issues) is $30.95.
You save $4.85 over the regular single copy price.
A limited number of the back issues are available separately at
$8.95, postpaid. Please include your name, mailing address, city,
state and zip code. Please make your check payable to *Porcupine*.
Porcupine
P.O. Box 259, Cedarburg, WI 53012
262-377-3962

REDDY & ASSOCIATES
IS LOOKING FOR A FEW GOOD NEW CLIENTS WHO CARE MORE ABOUT HUMANITY THAN THEY DO ABOUT THE BOTTOM LINE, MORE ABOUT TRUTH THAN SPIN, MORE ABOUT MEANING THAN INFORMATION....

WE AREN'T EXPECTING A LOT OF CALLS.

BUT LIFE IS SHORT AND WHAT YOU DO IN ORDER TO MAKE MONEY OUGHT TO BE FUN AND SHOULD LEAVE YOU AND THE WORLD BETTER AND STRONGER AT THE END OF EACH DAY.

IT'S A WORTHY GOAL FOR ANY GRAPHIC DESIGN PROJECT — GOOD PEOPLE, GOOD PLANNING, GOOD IDEAS, GOOD ARTWORK, GOOD RESULTS.

Tel: 262.377.8448 Fax: 262.377.9273 e-mail: reddy4life@aol.com

"There is hope in
honest error,

none in the
icy perfections
of a mere
stylist"

— Charles Rennie Mackintosh
Glasgow, 1901

Charles Radtke

Furniture Maker

W62 N732 Riveredge Drive ▪ Cedarburg, Wisconsin 53012

www.charlesradtke.com

(262) 375-8703

IF YOU ARE LOOKING FOR STILLNESS OR
TIME OUT OF TIME OR A PLACE TO
REST YOUR EYES OR SOMETHING TO PULL YOU
OUT OF—OR—INTO YOUR SELF

HAND-COLORED BLACK & WHITE PHOTOGRAPHIC IMAGES
AFRICA • CARIBBEAN • EUROPE • AMERICA

STUDIO SHOWING BY APPOINTMENT ONLY
262-377-1197

VICKI REED

P.O. Box 259 • Cedarburg, Wisconsin 53012
www.vickireed.com • Email: tinter8x10@aol.com